TRI-CITIES

Research by Barbara Kubik

Picture Research by Lindsay Johnson

"Partners in Progress" by Lisa Toomey
Produced in cooperation with
Tri-City Industrial Development Council

Windsor Publications, Inc.
Chatsworth, California

TRI-CITIES

The Mid-Columbia Hub

An Illustrated History by Ted Van Arsdol

Windsor Publications, Inc.—History Book
    Division
Managing Editor: Karen Story
Design Director: Alexander D'Anca
Photo Director: Susan L. Wells
Executive Editor: Pamela Schroeder

Staff for *Tri-Cities: The Mid-Columbia Hub*
Manuscript Editor: Susan M. Pahle
Photo Editor: Robin L. Sterling
Senior Editor, Corporate Biographies: Judith L.
    Hunter
Senior Production Editor, Corporate Biographies:
    Una Fitzsimons
Proofreader: Mary Jo Scharf
Customer Service Manager: Phyllis Feldman-
    Schroeder
Editorial Assistants: Kim Kievman, Michael
    Nugwynne, Michele Oakley, Kathy B. Peyser,
    Theresa J. Solis
Publisher's Representative, Corporate
    Biographies: David Cook
Designer: Thomas McTighe
Layout Artist: Bonnie Felt
Layout Artist, Corporate Biographies:
    Christopher L. Murray

Library of Congress Cataloging-in-Publication
    Data:
Van Arsdol, Ted.
Tri-cities : the Mid-Columbia hub / by Ted Van
    Arsdol. Partners in progress / by Lisa
    Toomey.
    p. 160 cm.22x28
    "Produced in cooperation with the Tri-City
    Industrial Development Council." Includes
    bibliographical references.
ISBN: 0-89781-345-6
    1. Pasco Region (Wash.)—History. 2. Pasco
    Region (Wash.)—Description and
    travel—Views. 3. Pasco Region
    (Wash.)—Industries. 4. Kennewick Region
    (Wash.)—History. 5. Kennewick Region
    (Wash.)—Description and travel—Views. 6.
    Kennewick Region (Wash.)—Industries. 7.
    Richland Region (Wash.)—History. 8.
    Richland Region (Wash.)—Description and
    travel—Views. 9. Richland Region
    (Wash.)—Industries. I. Toomey, Lisa.
    Partners in progress. 1990. II. Title.
F899.P37V36 1990
979.7'33—dc20   90-32883
                                   CIP

Windsor Publications, Inc.
Elliot Martin, Chairman of the Board
James L. Fish III, Chief Operating Officer
Michele Sylvestro, Vice President/Sales-
    Marketing
Mac Buhler, Vice President/Sponsor Acquisitions

▲ ▲ ▲

More than 5,000 spectators visited the Pasco Naval Air Station when the facility was opened to the public on Navy Day on October 27, 1945. Many fighter aircraft were displayed, and platforms were arranged so people could inspect the cockpits. Courtesy, Official U.S. Navy Photo

Contents

Acknowledgments

Many persons contributed to the completion of this book. The staffs of the following provided source material: Franklin County Historical Society, East Benton County Historical Society, Mid-Columbia Library in Kennewick and Pasco, Richland Public Library, Sacajawea Interpretive Center near Pasco, Tri-City Industrial Development Council, Fort Vancouver Regional Library at Vancouver, Oregon Historical Society at Portland, Seattle Public Library, the Washington State Library at Olympia, Webfooters Postcard Club at Portland, and the National Archives in Washington, D.C.

Appreciation also should be expressed by the author and by the research consultant, Barb Kubik, to Rudy Grazini, Merlene Willis, William Bequette, Bob Woehler, Jack Briggs, Elizabeth Miller, Mr. and Mrs. Bob Purcell, Phyllis Bowersock, Lloyd Aman, Walter Gary, Harold Garrett, Julia Anderson, Hec Hancock, and Mary Lindsay. Many others, too numerous to list, also obligingly answered questions about their fields of activity.

▲ ▲ ▲
Sunrise radiates over the still waters of the Columbia River. Photo by John Clement

This book is dedicated to my parents, Fred and Blanche Van Arsdol. My father was a patrol sergeant at Hanford during World War II.

CHAPTER ONE

Confluence of Three Rivers

▲ ▲ ▲

More than 100 years ago, the first settlers established an outpost at the confluence of three rivers—the mighty Columbia; its main tributary, the Snake; and the Yakima. All three are located in what is now southeastern Washington state. Initially the arid, barren appearance of the landscape didn't invite early travelers to linger. Nevertheless this junction played a major historical role in the exploration and settlement of the Pacific Northwest and more recently in the development of irrigation and nuclear projects in eastern Washington.

Situated at the confluence of these rivers are the present-day cities of Pasco, Richland, and Kennewick, collectively known as the Tri-Cities. Long before these cities ever existed, however, explorers traversed the area looking

for new areas to settle, fur traders gathered pelts from plentiful sources, and indigenous peoples worked and played on the sagebrush-covered land.

Archaeologists have uncovered remnants of this latter group by excavating areas around the Tri-Cities. Two of the more important excavation sites are the Windust caves near Lower Monumental Dam on the Snake River and the Marmes Rock Shelter at the junction of the Snake and Palouse rivers.

The excavations at Marmes uncovered skeletal remains beneath a layer of ash from Mount Mazama, a southern Oregon volcano that exploded 6,500 or more years ago and spread its debris over a wide region.

The quality and variety of items uncovered indicate the natives had established a stable culture, complete with leisure time, trade, and religious beliefs.

▲ ▲ ▲

Salmon was the principal source of food for the Columbia River tribes. The annual spring salmon run was celebrated with the festive "First Feast," which included prayers, rituals, songs, and feasting. As shown in this 1845 watercolor, the salmon were dried on open air racks for winter meals. The dusty desert winds added grit to the dried fish and, combined with the salmon bones, caused the Indian's teeth to be quite worn—a condition noted by early white visitors such as Lewis and Clark. Courtesy, Stark Museum of Art, Orange, Texas

On the Snake below Lower Monumental Dam, artifacts dated 4,500-9,000 years old have been found, which archaeologists believe were probably traded to the local Indian population. These artifacts include olivella shells from the Pacific coast, which were strung as beads; nephrite, a form of jade from British Columbia, which was used to make adz chisels; and obsidian from Glass Butte, Oregon, which was used to make arrowheads, spear points, and knives.

Archaeologists have also determined from remains that natives foraged for their survival, catching fish along the rivers during the migratory runs of salmon and steelhead; gathering seeds, roots, and berries; and hunting for game, sometimes in the mountains outside the river country. From other remains, archaeologists have learned that food resources were used for more than eating. For example, the natives used bird feathers for decoration and the bones for tools and ornaments. Some plants were gathered for basketry and other weaving, as well as for food.

Scientists have learned other things about these ancient Indian cultures from remains found at excavation sites. For instance, burials at Marmes are reported to have reflected a sense of community and religious beliefs, including a concern for an afterlife. Other remains left by these early residents include art, drawn on basalt cliffs along the Snake and Columbia. This and the items acquired in trade attest to a developed communication system among the early inhabitants.

About 2,000 years ago, some of the natives began clustering in winter villages with 50 or more tule-mat-covered pithouses on islands in the lower Snake and mid-Columbia rivers.

Much later, Indians established an important community at the Snake and Columbia junction. Fur trader Alexander Ross described the junction as a "great resort, or general rendezvous" for the Indians on important occasions. He called the junction of the Columbia and Snake the Grand or Great Forks.

John McLoughlin, Hudson's Bay Company's chief factor (main supervisor) at Fort Vancouver, referred to the place as the Nez Percé Forks for the Nez Percé Indians who inhabited the region. Another reference often used for the junction was Lewis and Clark Forks, named for the two U.S. Army captains who traveled down the Snake River in 1805.

In fact the first known whites to travel through the Tri-Cities area were the captains Meriwether Lewis and William Clark, who traveled with an expedition up the Missouri River in 1804, wintered in what is now North Dakota, and crossed the Bitterroot Range in 1805.

The Lewis and Clark expedition halted their canoes just above the mouth of "the River Kimooenim," or the Snake, on October 16, 1805, to smoke with Indians who had gathered in great numbers to view the newcomers. The Indians, called Sokulks by Lewis and Clark, lived in houses of large mats,

▲ ▲ ▲
This 1841 watercolor by Joseph Drayton, entitled **Fur Traders and Indians at Fort Walla Walla,** *accurately depicts the entrance of the fort of that period, but little else is a faithful portrayal. There were no trees, and the canoe and Indian clothing are not representative of the Cayuse, Nez Percé, or Walla Walla tribes that frequented the post. This oblong fort, made from driftwood, was large enough to corral some 100 horses. Timothy grass was gathered from the Yakima River delta to feed the stock. Courtesy, Oregon Historical Society*

made of rushes. On October 18, the party continued down the Columbia to the Pacific Ocean.

Returning from the Pacific Ocean in 1806, the Lewis and Clark expedition stopped at Chief Yellept's village, located west of the Columbia River about 10 miles downstream from the Snake at the mouth of the Walla Walla River. After the captains accepted the chief's invitation to stay another day, Sergeant Patrick Gass, a member of the expedition, reported that a hundred Indians from "the forks" joined the numerous other natives. Some of the expedition danced and sang with the Indians until late in the evening. In preparation for their remaining journey, the army expedition bought dogs for food, then crossed to the east bank of the Columbia and traveled overland to the Kooskooske (Clearwater) River.

The first British fur trader arriving in the area was David Thompson of the North West Company in July 1811. His canoe traveling down the Columbia stopped one-half mile above the Snake River at a large Indian camp, where he smoked with the men. Thompson informed them he was going to the ocean to get articles they needed and would return to trade for furs. The Indians suggested that Thompson set up a lodge near their camp for the promised trading. After camping overnight, the Thompson party traveled on July 9 to what is now the site of Sacajawea State Park and put up a small pole with a note attached, claiming the country for Great Britain and stating that his company intended "to erect a factory at this place for the commerce of the country around."

On his way back from the Columbia's mouth, Thompson stopped August 5-6 at the same Indian village, where 200 men resided in lodges with their families. Through an interpreter, Thompson reported his hopes that a trading ship would arrive by sea next year, and then explained he must first go to the mountains for goods. The Thompson party ascended the Snake River, and on August 9 stored its canoe at the mouth of Palouse River, acquired horses from Indians, and traveled north.

About the same time as Thompson's journeys, Americans also were involved in the first major trading efforts in the Pacific Northwest, east of the Cascade Mountains. In 1811, a Pacific Fur Company party sent out by an American, John Jacob Astor, established Fort Astoria at the Columbia's mouth near the Pacific Ocean, and in July 1812 an Astor party moved upriver. Near the mouth of the

▲ ▲ ▲

A common method of salmon fishing is pictured here in 1899 at the Celilo Falls on the Columbia River. Using long-handled nets, the Indians would stand on plank platforms constructed over the rushing rapids. Once the net was thrust upstream the rapids carried it downstream with the opening facing the fish. Courtesy, Oregon Historical Society

▲ ▲ ▲

Chief factor at Fort Vancouver from 1824 to 1846, Dr. John McLoughlin was an innovative, independent, and decisive manager, coordinating the multilingual and multinational fur trade for the Hudson's Bay Company. McLoughlin was known by a variety of names including "the Big Doctor," "White Headed Eagle," and the "Father of the Oregon Country." Courtesy, Oregon Historical Society

Walla Walla River, the fur traders bought horses for a small party led by Robert Stuart, which started for the Blue Mountains on a long trip to St. Louis, Missouri.

The remaining fur traders spent three days camped on the north side of the Snake, probably close to where Thompson had stopped, and purchased more horses. Some then proceeded up the river to establish a trading post in the Snake River country. Part of the brigade traveled in boats and others dragged canoes on land, which was "very difficult," reported Ross Cox, one of the group. Another party, which included Alexander Ross and leader David Stuart (the uncle of Robert Stuart) departed in canoes up the Columbia toward Fort Okanogan located about 150 miles north.

En route, they met a tall, middle-aged Indian named "Ha-qui-laugh," which Ross thought was a Sahaptin word meaning doctor or priest. The fur trappers also noted Indians were participating in sprinkling rituals and other ceremonies that seemed like an imitation of Catholic church rites. Because of these incidents the travelers called the nearby rapids Priest Rapids.

Astor's venture proved to be ill-fated. The destruction of his ship *Tonquin* at Nootka Sound, inadequate fur returns, and other problems hampered the venture. The War of 1812 with Great Britain left Fort Astoria in an exposed, precarious position. In 1813, the fort was sold to the North West Company, thus ending the Pacific Fur Company's endeavors in the region. The post was renamed Fort George.

In April 1814 the Astor party departed from Fort George in 10 canoes on a journey up the Columbia that eventually would take them overland through Canada to Montreal, a trip requiring nearly five months.

On April 15, while traveling on the Columbia a short distance north of the Yakima River mouth, the Astor party noticed some canoes desperately trying to reach them and heard a child's voice shouting in French, "Stop! Stop!" The travelers pulled ashore, and the canoes, which contained Walla Walla Indians, joined the traders. Among the new arrivals were the two children and Iowa Indian wife of Pierre Dorion, a hunter who had been in a group of nine men sent to get supplies from the Snake Indians.

Apparently while Dorion and the other men had been scattered throughout the countryside setting out beaver traps, they had been attacked and killed by Indians, although one had survived long enough to reach Mrs. Dorion and inform her of the tragedy. She fled with her two children on two horses into the

Blue Mountains and spent the winter. The mother killed the horses for food, then crossed the mountains to the Columbia after the food supply was exhausted. Walla Walla Indians took in the three survivors, awaiting the canoes they knew would arrive from upriver in the spring.

Now that the Astorians were gone, the North West Company controlled the fur trade business east of the Cascades with a varied and colorful aggregation of employees, consisting of Great Britain natives, Kanakas (Hawaiians), Iroquois Indians, and others.

▲ ▲ ▲

The various Indian tribes of the Columbia Plateau viewed sweathouses as a place of spiritual renewal and purification. Their feelings about this cleansing ritual have been compared to the sense of awe imbued by the great cathedrals of Europe. Courtesy, U.S. Army Corps of Engineers, Walla Walla District

Ross Cox told about one company brigade traveling up the Columbia in two barges and nine canoes in 1817. At the mouth of the Walla Walla River, the travelers bought horses from the Indians. This kind of commerce would continue for a long time at the same place. One party split off for a trip up the Snake to the country of the Shoshone, while the others, in loaded canoes, continued up the Columbia. At Priest Rapids another party left and headed for the Rocky Mountains.

According to Alexander Ross, a company employee, some Indian villages that the traders passed by in 1817 "had upwards of a thousand inhabitants," especially around the Great Forks or Grand Forks. This was the largest number of Indians he saw along the rivers in any year.

In July 1818, Donald McKenzie arrived with a brigade on the Walla Walla River to establish a fort and prepare an expedition to the upper Snake River country. McKenzie departed in September, leaving Alexander Ross to complete the new Fort Nez Percés. Ross later graphically described the fort's beginnings and his problems in diplomacy with the Indians in *Fur Hunters of the Far West*.

Ross was clerk until 1823 at this fort on the Columbia River, which was located just north of the mouth of the Walla Walla River about 10 miles downstream from the Snake. The fort was then controlled by the Hudson's Bay Company; the North West and Hudson's Bay companies merged in 1821.

Among the better-known Hudson's Bay employees was John Work, who kept detailed records of his travels. In 1824, while returning downriver with seven boats "loaded with Snake and Thompson's River veterans," Work mentioned the country near the Snake and Columbia junction was "covered with great quantities of wormwood, but scarcely a tree to be seen." (The "veterans" were men who had survived the arduous Snake River and Thompson expeditions, and the wormwood was probably sagebrush.) Twice in 1824 Work returned upriver and each time crossed the sandy, windy plains from Fort Nez Percés to the Snake River, then traveled up the Snake to the Palouse River en route to the Spokane River. At one time, he wrote "we were like to be choked by dust."

▲ ▲ ▲

ABOVE: Analyzing the supply needs of the North West Company fur trade in the interior Columbia region, Alexander Ross recognized and promoted the strategic location of the Snake, Walla Walla, and Columbia rivers confluence. He recommended moving Spokane House to that site, but the contrast between the attractive environment near Spokane and the bleakness of the Wallula Gap area made Spokane House traders resist the move. Courtesy, Oregon Historical Society

Another well-known employee was the Hudson's Bay Company's governor, George Simpson. He recognized that the Americans might succeed in establishing a claim to the land south of the Snake River. If this happened, Simpson planned to have the fort torn down, rafted across the Snake, and rebuilt.

In a visit to the fort in 1824, Simpson learned only 2,000 beaver hides had been taken in during the season. Simpson also noted that the Indians were "very independent," coming in for company supplies only when in absolute need.

Simpson arrived back upriver in March 1825, shortly after christening Fort Vancouver, far down the Columbia. He conferred at Fort Nez Percés with Indian chiefs and 300 warriors and gave them presents. Simpson also had brought up 10 bushels of seed potatoes. He hoped the potatoes would largely replace the imported provisions and the numerous butchered horses that had been eaten at the fort in the past.

After continuing upriver, Simpson's men had to go ashore numerous times along the west side of present-day Franklin County for scraps of wood to burn in the evening. At Priest Rapids they encountered low water, which resulted in poling, hauling, and walking their canoes and supplies up the river.

Simpson did not see a single tree along the Columbia between The Dalles and the area north of today's Vantage. He described this stretch of land as "the most sterile tract country perhaps in North America." He did not mention a rather stunted juniper forest growing about 15 miles northeast of the Snake River's mouth; this was hidden from the view of the Columbia River travelers. Part of this curious forest, in what may be the largest sand dunes in Washington state, has survived and is now managed by the U.S. Bureau of Land Management.

The Hudson's Bay voyagers had become familiar with a long line of bluffs on the east side of the Columbia above Yakima River after passing by them many times. The bluffs were called the Marl Banks, or White Bluffs—the French Canadians referred to them as "les Terres Jaunes." The mountains to the southeast, visible for many miles from the site of the Tri-Cities, were called "les Montagnes Bleues"; later the English translation "Blue Mountains" was used and is still in use today. A French name, the Pavilion River, was applied to the present Palouse River, upstream from the Grand Forks.

The natives had grown accustomed to the company boats that passed by their villages regularly; among the boats was an "express." An "express" ordinarily consisted of several bateaux, or canoes, manned by Indians or French Canadians. Customarily one express traveled upstream each year, bound for eastern

Canada, and another traveled downstream to Fort Vancouver. The transcontinental journey across Canada required about six months, and occasionally a second express would be dispatched each way during the year.

In an 1829 dispatch, Simpson admitted Fort Nez Percés was "not very productive" and the area not rich, but the Hudson's Bay Company needed the post to accommodate the Indians, whether the fort was productive or not. Expeditions to the Snake country could not pass through if the company was not on good terms with Indians of the middle Columbia River area. Also, the company had to acquire about 250 Indian horses annually. Simpson noted that the fur trade, mostly with the Cayuse Indians, paid "tolerably well."

Peter Skene Ogden was another notable individual connected with Fort Nez Percés history. He had led Snake River expeditions since 1824. In 1830 he led a pelt-gathering expedition that reflected the Hudson's Bay Company's heavy need for horses from the Indians. A total of 272 horses and mules, partly loaded with provisions, were taken along. Personnel totaled 115; there were 38 men plus women and children. Before returning to the fort in late July 1831, the expedition reached as far as what is now Nevada, and traveled more than 2,000 miles.

John Work, a member of this expedition as well, said those groups who were seeking beaver, were in constant danger of capture by ruthless savages, aside from encountering hardships of various other kinds.

Potential problems with Indians in large areas of the Northwest diminished about this same time as the result of the deadly epidemics of 1830-1831; the epidemics included smallpox, measles, dysentery, and general fevers. As many

▲ ▲ ▲

ABOVE: English botanist David Douglas traveled extensively throughout the Pacific Northwest in the late 1820s, discovering new species of plants on both sides of the Cascade Mountains. His journals note a number of birds in the mid-Columbia region and a variety of new plant specimens along the Columbia River shoreline. Courtesy, Oregon Historical Society

ABOVE, RIGHT: Peter Skene Ogden joined the Hudson's Bay Company when it merged with the North West Company in 1821. Under his leadership, expeditions of trappers, traders, and their households journeyed up the Columbia River to the Snake River area where they bravely endured limited provisions, dust storms, heat, and hostile Indians. In 1827 he wrote "this life makes a young man sixty in a few years." Courtesy, Oregon Historical Society

as 80 percent of the Northwest's Indians are believed to have died; below Celilo Falls the fatality rate may have been 90 percent.

Also in the 1830s, the possibility of gaining numerous Christian converts among the surviving Indians had aroused the interest of ministers. Several of them crossed the Plains to establish missions.

In early September 1834, Methodist missionary Jason Lee stopped at Fort Nez Percés briefly, about the same time as Nathaniel Wyeth of the Columbia River Fishing and Trading Company. Reverend Samuel Parker arrived at the fort from the Nez Percé country in 1835. His first sight was of grazing cattle. Parker wrote, "I never felt more joy in entering a habitation of civilized people."

In 1836 Parker returned upriver in a bateaux, stayed at the fort two weeks, and preached to numerous Cayuse, Walla Walla, and Nez Percé Indians. He and Pierre C. Pambrun, who was in charge of Fort Nez Percés, rode 10 miles to the mouth of the Lewis or Nez Percé River, now known as the Snake River. "The soil is good, as evidenced by the fresh verdure, which is springing up luxuriantly, at this early season," Parker observed. Parker made his observation during May, when vegetation is often green before drying out in the summer heat.

The first white women, Narcissa Whitman and Eliza Hart Spalding, arrived from a long, tiring westward journey in September 1836 with their husbands, Marcus Whitman and Henry Harmon Spalding, who were missionaries. As the Whitmans passed a vegetable garden two miles east of the fort, the long journey's fatigues were forgotten "in the excitement of being so close," Mrs. Whitman wrote. At the fort, Mrs. Whitman was delighted by cushioned arm chairs and a meal of fresh salmon, potatoes, tea, bread and butter, even delighted by the cheery crow of a rooster perched on a doorstep. The sight of chickens, turkeys, pigeons, cows, goats, and swine in the fort grounds also was nostalgic. The missionaries continued downriver, but later the Whitmans returned to Walla Walla Valley and the Spaldings settled among Nez Percé Indians at Lapwai.

Catholic missionaries were not far behind. In 1838, Catholic fathers Modeste Demers and Francis Norbert Blanchet arrived at the fort from upriver with the express. They held mass and baptized several persons before continuing downriver, and in 1839 Demers visited Fort Walla Walla (the former Fort Nez Percés) and Fort Colville, another Hudson's Bay Company post, in what is now northeastern Washington.

This same year Pambrun died at Fort Walla Walla after a fall from a horse.

▲ ▲ ▲
According to the Hudson's Bay Company archives, the wall around Fort Walla Walla stood 12 feet high and was more than one foot thick as depicted in this 1846 Paul Kane watercolor. The enclosed area was 113 feet by 113 feet and included two dwelling structures, one row of houses for men, one row of stores, a powder magazine, one pigeon house, a poultry coop, and two bastions. Courtesy, Stark Museum of Art, Orange, Texas

Chief Factor John McLoughlin termed Pambrun "a most able manager . . . in one of the most difficult places to manage in the Indian country." Pambrun had been at the fort since 1832.

Another unfortunate event, in late 1841, was the burning of the fort. Archibald McKinlay rebuilt the post of adobe, or unbaked bricks, completing the project in 1842.

A short distance south, the flood of U.S. immigrants over the Oregon Trail to the Willamette Valley was increasing in the 1840s, and some took a sidetrip to Fort Walla Walla. In October 1843, explorer John C. Frémont saw immigrants directed by Jesse Applegate building Mackinaw boats at the fort to continue down the Columbia. But many of the immigrants bypassed the fort and continued a land journey along the Columbia with livestock and wagons.

Indians were getting concerned about what the future held for them as the number of whites increased. Joel Palmer headed through the Great Plains, traveled to the fort in 1846, and discovered that the Walla Walla chief, Peopeomoxmox or Yellow Serpent, was "not very friendly." Americans had killed his son in California during the previous year.

But the fort continued its important role a while longer. The Reverend Pierre-Jean De Smet, a Jesuit, loaded supplies at the fort for his mission in 1846; he had visited there previously. In 1847, the fort became the seat of the Bishop of Walla Walla. Bishop A.M.A. Blanchet arrived from the Great Plains, and one historian says Blanchet was "astonished" to see his forlorn headquarters. He established missions on the Umatilla River and in the Yakima Valley.

Times got considerably more troubled near the end of 1847 when the Cayuse Indians killed Marcus and Narcissa Whitman and other whites at the mission in the Walla Walla Valley about 20 miles east of the fort. Peter Skene Ogden traveled upriver from Fort Vancouver to Fort Walla Walla to offer a ransom for 52 women and children who were being held captive by the Indians

▲ ▲ ▲

Pictured here as they confer about the state of Catholic religion in the Pacific Northwest around 1870 are, from left to right, A.M.A. Blanchet, F. Norbert Blanchet, and Modeste Demers. All three priests traveled throughout the mid-Columbia region in the 1800s, introducing the Catholic faith to the Indians, and tending to the spiritual needs of early Catholic settlers. A.M.A. Blanchet served as the first bishop of Walla Walla at Fort Walla Walla prior to being appointed first bishop of western Washington. Courtesy, Oregon Historical Society

▲ ▲ ▲

This circa 1825 drawing by Alexander Ross depicts the original Fort Nez Percés, reflecting the feelings of isolation experienced by the early fur traders. Ross called the fort "the strongest and most complete fort west of the Rocky Mountains . . . the Gibraltar of Columbia." The fort walls were 20 feet high and 6 inches thick with an 18-inch-square window through which trade with the local Indians was conducted. Courtesy, Oregon Historical Society

at Waiilatpu in the Walla Walla Valley. The Indians delivered the hostages to Fort Walla Walla; later the women and children were moved to safer areas downriver.

While most travelers arriving at the fort continued down the Columbia River, one group consisting of 36 wagons ferried across the stream and traveled up the Yakima Valley, then crossed the Cascade Mountains in 1853. James Longmire said the immigrants bought driftwood from the Hudson's Bay Company to make a flatboat ferry for their goods at the Columbia. Indians in canoes swam the horses and cattle across. Longmire recalled the chief, Yellow Serpent, was riding a beautiful American bay horse "with the dignity of a king." Holsters on his saddle contained a pair of U.S. Navy revolvers.

In 1853 and 1854, parties involved in explorations and surveys for a railroad to the Pacific Coast traveled through the area. Isaac Stevens, Washington Territory governor, was in general command. One party, led by James Doty, traveled up the Yakima River in 1854; Doty reported an extensive fish weir in the vicinity of what was later called Horn Rapids.

The fort, now generally known as Fort Walla Walla, finally was abandoned in 1855 when war broke out with the Indians. Plympton Kelly, of the Oregon Mounted Regiment, wrote that his unit advanced with caution when they saw crows flying and lighting on the deserted fort. The place had been looted, and even floorboards had been ripped up by natives seeking anything of value. The war dragged on into the following year. Yellow Serpent was killed in 1856 while reportedly trying to escape from the custody of volunteer soldiers.

The fort's closure ended the Hudson's Bay era in the Tri-Cities area. Earlier,

in 1846, the British had dropped their claim to much of the region in a treaty with the United States setting the boundary between this country and Canada at the 49th parallel.

Some of the former fur company employees had settled in the Walla Walla Valley. The French-Canadian community in this area became known as Frenchtown.

Most of the area's Indians were forced onto reservations. One small group that never signed a treaty was the Wanapum of the Priest Rapids area, who practiced some of their customs into recent years.

Johnny Buck, leader of the band at the time the Hanford reservation was established, said the Wanapums fished at traditional places on the Columbia and Snake rivers and also gathered roots and berries. They supplemented their income with part-time work for farmers, such as picking hops in the Yakima Valley.

The Wanapums lived in homes covered with tule mats. When food gathering slowed in the winter, the women wove cattail and tule mats for bedding, tables, lodging covers, and burials and worked on baskets. The men worked stone into knives, scrapers, and other implements, commented Delores Buck of the Wanapums in a 1984 interview.

The federal government's takeover of a large area for Hanford in 1943 closed off some sites that were considered sacred by the Indians. But the U.S. Department of Energy has made some allowance for this problem, by occasionally permitting Yakima and Wanapum Indians onto Gable Mountain for religious observances.

▲ ▲ ▲

Two members of the Wanapum tribe are pictured here in the late 1940s constructing a traditional tule mat lodge. Used as summer dwellings by plateau Indian tribes in the mid-Columbia region for centuries, these lodges could be expanded in size and relocated as needed. Photo by Click Relander. Courtesy, Ted Van Arsdol

CHAPTER TWO

Navigation and Locomotion

▲ ▲ ▲

A correspondent of the *Walla Walla Daily Journal* wrote in 1884: "Last night, six veritable Chinese junks, by means of sails, oars and poles, were gotten past our town on their way up the river to pan out gold dust from the sandbars." The sight of gold seekers was frequent from the mid-1850s into the 1890s.

A gold rush in 1855 brought hundreds from the Willamette Valley in Oregon to the Colville area in the northeast Washington Territory, but results were sparse for most. One prospector, John Kerns, who passed old Fort Walla Walla, said he heard rumors of trouble with Indians and finally returned downriver in September from Colville, "disgusted with the idea of starting again both in regard to scenery and safety." Killings by Indians and other

troubles with the natives—who believed their treaties were being violated—held back the gold hunting from late in 1855 into 1857.

In 1858 the discovery of gold on the Fraser River of British Columbia touched off a stampede from California and Oregon Territory. Again, numerous parties traveled up the Columbia River, and some passed through what is now the Tri-Cities area. Hostile tribes, objecting to the influx of people east of the Cascade Mountains, were defeated in 1858 in two battles near Spokane, and the way was cleared for settlement and mining exploration in eastern Washington Territory.

Walla Walla was established in 1858, 30 miles east of the old Hudson's Bay Company's post, Fort Walla Walla; the U.S. Army built its own Fort Walla

Walla near the new town.

Routine steamboat travel started in 1859. One of the first steamboats in the area, the *Colonel Wright*, was launched at the mouth of the Deschutes River in late 1858. Then it traveled to Priest Rapids on the Columbia and also pioneered into the Snake, ascending to the mouth of Tucannon River; both trips were taken in 1859.

In 1859 and 1860, miners' interest was focused on the Similkameen mines in British Columbia. Gold was also discovered in 1860 in what is now central Idaho, and a major rush was under way there by late 1861.

Walla Walla boomed as an important supply town on the Nez Percé Trail, which led to the Clearwater River. From the Clearwater, supplies could easily be transported to the mines. Steamboat cargo and passengers for Walla Walla were unloaded at Wallula, established in 1862 at the site of the old Fort Walla Walla. The firm of Vansyckle and Tatem operated a hotel at Wallula, advertising "clean beds and no bugs" and a hay yard. Pack animals were loaded at Wallula for long overland trips to the mines, first to Idaho Territory (split away from Washington Territory in 1863) and later over the Bitterroot Range to Montana mining camps.

In 1863 miners worked Columbia River sandbars near Priest Rapids and at Ringgold Bar, about 25 miles upstream from the site of Pasco. Ringgold (now spelled Ringold) was said to have been named for one of the miners.

Numerous other miners were merely traveling through, toward northern Idaho and Montana—so many that a steamboat town called White Bluffs, nearly 30 miles above present-day Richland on the east bank of the Columbia, was active in the mid-1860s. Several buildings and tents comprised another community, Ringgold City, in 1866, located 15 miles below White Bluffs.

The first Caucasian miners on sandbars in the vicinity soon gave up prospecting, but Chinese moved in. The Chinese were satisfied with "diggings," which paid less than others wanted, and during the late 1860s through the 1880s, great numbers of Chinese—frequently several thousand a year—were scattered along the Columbia and Snake, working on numerous sandbars in addition to working mining camps in central Idaho. They ranged as far up the rivers as Hells Canyon on the Idaho and Oregon border and the Okanogan area of Central Washington.

In the late 1860s, 75 to 100 Chinese wintered annually at Wallula. Four Chinese arriving in 1866 from upriver reported that their two companions and all their gold dust and mining equipment were lost in rapids while they were coming down from a mining area at Rock Island. The survivors were garbed only in pants made of flour sacks. Wallula residents donated old hats, boots, and shoes to the new arrivals.

Meanwhile many more Chinese were heading upriver. In 1866 a steamer arrived in Wallula that "looked like she had gone into the coolie trade," a newspaper report commented. Stages and wagons were loaded with Chinese.

Hollis Conover, cowboy for cattleman Dave Coonc, recalled that 100 to 200 Chinese mined gold in the late 1870s opposite Ringold Bar. They came upriver in the fall and mined during low water through the late winter. "I would hear those rockers all day and night, as long as they could see to do anything," Conover said. He remembered a string of miners pulling an old flatboat upriver, with others aboard steering. At the time, cattlemen lived in the buildings at White Bluffs, where old freight roads of the 1860s on the east bank still were plainly visible.

Newspaper reports from this time mentioned that Chinese on the Snake and Columbia rivers burrowed into holes in the ground; brush and earth kept out the rain. For cooking, the miners gathered driftwood. Despite the makeshift dwellings reported in the newspaper, the Chinese miners did establish self-sufficient camps and settlements along the river's edge. The Chinese were their own doctors, carpenters, cooks, and farmers; their gardens were so successful that they frequently sold produce to white settlers. One of the largest of these settlements was located at the confluence of the Columbia and the Chelan rivers.

▲ ▲ ▲

After working for the railroads or mining for gold, many Chinese immigrants settled in small towns throughout the Pacific Northwest, maintaining their traditional lifestyles while starting service businesses like grocery stores, restaurants, and laundries. Local newspapers, however, added to the already rampant racism by referring to the Chinese people as the "Yellow Peril," and the "heathen Chinee." Courtesy, Idaho State Historical Society

Steamboats continued to carry cargo and passengers up the Snake River past the site of the Tri-Cities to Lewiston in high-water periods, although business was not as good as in the early 1860s. Below the Snake, the two main landings in the 1860s were Wallula and Umatilla, where pack trains and wagons loaded up with cargo from the lower Columbia.

Much of the trade from Wallula went through Walla Walla. But one pack train trail, heavily promoted in 1867 as the best route from Wallula to the Montana mines, extended through what is now eastern Franklin County. From Wallula, this "Washtucna Road" ran across sagebrush land to Fishhook Bend on the Snake River, followed old Indian trails to Jim Ford's Island 10 miles further upriver, then went up a hill and on to Washtucna (now Kahlotus) Lake in a bunchgrass-rich coulee, once a well-traveled Indian route.

Spring was the busiest time at the landings, when the steamboats resumed navigation. The boats did not operate in winter when the river iced up or

▲ ▲ ▲

Captain John C. Ainsworth was one of the three owners of the Oregon Steam Navigation Company, which held the first transportation monopoly on the Columbia River. The high freight rates frustrated citizens of the Washington Territory, yet they may have been necessary to support the expensive system. Courtesy, Oregon Historical Society

froze over. In 1868 Wallula packers celebrated renewed activity with a dance, described in the *Walla Walla Statesman.*

It was none of your paper-collar, patent leather boot arrangements but a jovial surprise party, where the bone and muscle of the country come together for a few hours' enjoyment; one of those parties where, when a gentleman is introduced to a lady and asks her to dance, it is not required to give his pedigree or show cause why his father and uncles are not exempt bondholders . . . We went through the whole calendar of dances from plain to fancy.

Pack animals faced growing competition as roads improved and more wagons entered the freighting business. Much of the trade at Umatilla, a major supply point for southern Idaho, ended in 1869 after construction of the Central Pacific Railroad through northern Nevada, which brought southern Idaho in easy reach of trains. Pack train commerce from Wallula to various mining camps and other destinations continued in the early 1870s but on a smaller scale than in the 1860s. In 1876, several of the last pack animals were taken to British Columbia to haul supplies for mines there.

But Wallula remained an important stopping place for the steamboats. And in 1878 one steamboat brought General O.O. Howard, U.S. Army commanding officer for the region, to confer at Priest Rapids with Chief Moses, of the Sinkiuse Indians. Moses was a prominent Indian leader who had chosen to remain at peace with white settlers, unlike the Paiute, Bannock, and Nez Percé Indians who went on the warpath. During the Indian uprisings, settlers were alarmed that Moses would join in, and rumors were circulated that some of his Indians had taken part in killing a couple named Perkins. The death of the couple caused quite a sensation at the time, and Moses was captured by a posse and jailed for awhile.

By the 1870s, newly arrived ranchers were using much of the unfenced range for their open-range cattle herds. A.L. Flint, living at the time at Parker Bottom on the Yakima River, said the range south of the Columbia between Priest Rapids and the Cold Springs vicinity was a favorite winter range. In the big spring roundup, cattlemen took along pack horses with provisions and bedding for a week or two on the range. The wide-roaming cattle were driven to Yakima River ranches for branding.

Then the cowboys drove the herds to summer range in Kittitas Valley, "cow heaven," west of the Columbia River. There the herds were relatively close to the small towns of Puget Sound, an important market in the 1870s, and could be driven across the mountains to be sold.

Starting about 1875, Midwest buyers began visiting the area, buying herds to drive east through southern Idaho and Wyoming. Cowboy Milt Burge participated in one drive from Yakima Valley to the Columbia around 1879 for transfer to Lang and Ryan, one of the biggest cattle outfits. "We drove 400 to

▲ ▲ ▲
The Richland Transfer company profited from the coming of the railroad by hauling crates, boxes of merchandise, and other items to Richland through what is now Columbia Park. Owner W.S. Muncey bought his first gasoline truck in 1917 and was so impressed with this transportation improvement that he completely motorized his operation by 1918, putting 14 teams of horses out to pasture. Courtesy, East Benton County Historical Society

600 head to White Bluffs," he remembered. "Indians in canoes guided the herd across to the other shore—it was a long way."

Among several cattlemen with headquarters near the mouth of Yakima River was Ben Rosencrance, who operated a stage coach station in the 1880s. Rosencrance, who arrived in the late 1870s, eventually acquired land at the site of Richland that was used to develop a town in the early 1900s.

One of the major owners of horses among Indians in the Pasco vicinity was Harlish Washomake (Wolf Necklace) of the Palouse tribe, generally known among the settlers as Chief Wolf. News reports said his choicest horses were of an unusual breed, blue colored and very graceful. Wolf would not divulge their origin to inquisitive settlers.

Raising horses and cattle was advantageous to early settlers of the area because herds could be driven to distant markets. Travel by horse or wagon continued as the best means of transportation until the arrival of railroads.

The first rail line east of a Cascades portage road was built by the Walla Walla and Columbia River Railroad Company, linking Wallula with Walla Walla. Timber to help construct this project was rafted from the upper Yakima River to a Wallula steam sawmill in the early 1870s. Crews had difficulty getting logs out of Grande Ronde River, a Snake River tributary, and timber from there did not arrive until 1875. The new railroad was completed to Touchet in 1874 and to Walla Walla in 1875. According to John Murphy, who wrote *Rambles in North-western America*, published in 1879, the trains were so slow moving that drivers of big freight wagons drawn by seven or eight pairs of mules and horses or by numerous oxen would challenge the train to a race on its wooden tracks. But the engineer "scorned their insinuations."

A much bigger railroad project, involving the Northern Pacific Railroad (NPRR), was preceded by the laying out of a town at the Snake River's mouth in the summer of 1879. This was named for John Ainsworth, head of Oregon Steam Navigation Company. Machinery for a mill was delivered to the shore to help cut timber for railroad construction. Eventually two mills were active there.

▲ ▲ ▲

Payroll statistics from the Northern Pacific construction accounts show that in the summer of 1880 about half of the labor force was Chinese, the other being white. Chinese muscle did most of the backbreaking work as this photograph of a Chinese railroad gang in 1890 by F. Jay Haynes documents. Courtesy, Haynes Foundation Collection, Montana Historical Society

▲ ▲ ▲

The Oregon River and Navigation Company built a switchyard and roundhouse in Wallula to fuel, water, and repair train engines at this division point. Situated close to the two rivers, high water was a common problem for Wallula residents. In 1894 it flooded the houses and covered the railroad yard. Courtesy, Oregon Historical Society

On September 30, a steamboat pulled out from Wallula with W.H. McCartney, the NPRR's assistant general superintendent, and a large group of mechanics and laborers aboard, bound for the new town. Wallula residents were so excited by the prospect of having a railroad in the area, they shouted and cheered. General John W. Sprague, the NPRR's general manager, turned the first shovelful of dirt October 2 at Ainsworth, and NPRR workers began grading to the north to Spokane, Washington.

The company planned to construct the line through Spokane and over the Bitterroot Range in Idaho. Eventually, in 1883, the eastern end of this track linked with the NPRR line constructed westward from Minnesota.

Track iron and other materials for construction were transported on the Columbia River by steamboat and over two portages by railroad. Wood was rafted down Yakima River to Ainsworth and also down the Clearwater River of central Idaho into the Snake.

The first construction locomotive that ran out of Ainsworth was the *Otter Tail*, which was used for NPRR track construction near Duluth, Minnesota, and also used to haul iron for construction on Northern Pacific's Kalama-Tacoma line in the early 1870s. Jack Cartwright, NPRR employee, explained that the *Otter Tail* burned wood. Railroad employees gathered driftwood, cut it into two-foot lengths, and then burned it in the locomotive. Sagebrush was good

fuel material as well. Cartwright noted extra large sagebrush grew at the Pasco site; "it made good fire and lots of steam."

Getting water to men and teams, who were grading the desert land, was a problem. Much of the time wells dug by construction areas failed to produce water. The first good well north of Pasco, at what is now Eltopia, was called "the 21-mile well." Teams hauled water from there to the scattered crews.

At first railroad ties were acquired from the Walla Walla and Columbia River Railroad, but logs soon were arriving at booms on the Snake and Columbia for the Ainsworth mill, which cut lumber at a rate of 65-80,000 board feet per day. Log drives from the upper Yakima River continued in the early 1880s, in addition to the use of logs arriving from the Clearwater.

In 1880, flatcars and boxcars were shipped from Tacoma over the NPRR line and upriver to Ainsworth, then assembled for use on the new route. Locomotives, which were shipped up the Columbia, also arrived in 1880 from the East. Meantime, hundreds of men—mostly Chinese and Irish—continually moved the railroad towards Spokane by grading the land and laying track.

At the same time that the NPRR was laying track, the Oregon Railway and Navigation Company (OR&N) embarked on major construction at and near the Columbia River. One main objective was to build a line on the south bank of the river in Oregon, which would connect with Ainsworth. By the end of 1880, Ainsworth and Wallula were linked by rail. The OR&N also had rebuilt the old railroad east of Wallula and was extending a line from Walla Walla toward the Snake River and Palouse country.

Residents at Wallula and Ainsworth huddled around stoves during the severe winter of 1880-81. In the outlying country, a large percentage of the

▲ ▲ ▲

Henry Villard's desire to connect the Columbia Gateway to eastern markets was instrumental in extending the Northern Pacific Railroad through the mid-Columbia region to Portland, Oregon. Fearful that the Northern Pacific line would cross the Cascades and reduce the profitability of the Oregon Railroad and Navigation Company, Villard and his friends secretly purchased 60 percent of Northern Pacific common stock in 1880. Pictured here in 1895, Villard controlled both companies by 1881. Courtesy, Oregon Historical Society

wide-ranging cattle herds perished. Between Mesa and Eagle Rock, north of present-day Pasco, hundreds of animals died by drifting with the wind and falling off cliffs into the rocks and deep snowdrifts. Seeking shelter, cattle broke into homestead shacks nearer the Columbia, while hundreds of other cattle drifted with the bitter winds and wandered onto river ice, broke through, and drowned. Numerous cattlemen went out of business in the following spring. Some began raising horses. Nine years later another severe winter caused more heavy losses to open-range livestock.

In 1881 a steamboat, the *Frederick K. Billings*, constructed at Celilo for $35,000, arrived at Ainsworth to haul freight between the two banks of the Snake. Later the boat ferried trains across the river, after inclines were completed in 1882. The inclines extended from the riverbank down to the edge of the river, so that trains could run from the main track to the river, then board the ferry and resume passage on the other side. In about 30 minutes, the captain of the *Billings*, William P. Gray, would load an eight-car train onto the ferry and take his cargo to the other side of the river.

Ainsworth, home mostly to railroad workers, contained a boarding house, stables, a carpenter shop, railway offices, a 10-stall roundhouse, several sawmills, and numerous shops, including a butcher, dairy, and several stores

▲ ▲ ▲

Inclines on both sides of the Snake River made it possible to load trains onto the **Frederick K. Billings** *transfer steamer. It took five minutes for the train to be loaded and about 15-20 minutes for the steamboat to cross the river. Rooftops from the town of Ainsworth (right) and the construction dredges for the railroad bridge (left) are also visible in this 1883 photograph by F. Jay Haynes. Courtesy, Haynes Foundation Collection, Montana Historical Society*

carrying general merchandise. In addition it is said that Ainsworth contained "one house of vice per 10 inhabitants!" Those houses of vice included gambling, prostitution, saloons, and opium dens.

Francis H. Cook, a Spokane editor who visited Ainsworth in 1881 claimed the town could, "boast of a few of the best people, the largest amount of bad men and women and the greatest amount of sin, dust, and general disagreeableness of any place of its size on the coast." Another newspaper writer found gambling saloons in "full blast," day and night.

Vigilantes burned an opium den in 1881, which may have stirred a resident named "Black Dick" to knife a bystander several times in the back at the fire scene, severely wounding him. Vigilantes took the knifer out of jail in the night and lynched him. Later they ordered other unwanted characters out of town.

It should be pointed out that the town also contained a schoolhouse, a church, a cemetery, and a post office.

In 1882 crews began work on a railroad bridge at Ainsworth on the Snake River. Iron for the drawbridge arrived from Pennsylvania, and stone for piers was quarried from Granite Point on the Snake River above Penawawa. The stone was shipped down the Snake in barges, or if the water level was low, it was carried over the 0R&N line from Texas Ferry (Riparia) through Wallula. Starting in 1883, some of the needed stone was transported over the new NPRR line from quarries at Lake Pend Oreille, Idaho.

A special train arrived in Ainsworth in September 1883 carrying dignitaries who had participated in the Golden Spike ceremony in Montana, linking the two ends of NPRR track. Two hundred passengers stayed in the area most of the day. Henry Gantenbein, living west of Ainsworth, treated the visitors to locally raised watermelons. The train continued to Portland over the new 0R&N line for a big celebration. Also in September, the first shipment over the NPRR from the west coast to the east—11 cars of salmon—passed through Ainsworth.

In late 1883, a new railroad line was opened from Palouse Junction (Connell) to Endicott and Colfax in Whitman County. The line had been built eastward from the main Northern Pacific track. But more importantly for the Ainsworth area, railroad track was laid west of the Columbia, on a route that extended into the Yakima Valley and later to Puget Sound.

The steamboat, *Spokane*, carried rails, ties, and other materials to Cottonwood Landing on the Columbia's west bank, a few miles above Ainsworth, and graders moved west on a 25-mile contract. This new NPRR effort seemed to assure that an important permanent community would be developed at or near the river crossing.

As if in anticipation of the impending changes, Washington Territorial legislators established Franklin County in 1883; this area had formerly been part of Whitman County. Ainsworth was designated as the Franklin County seat in late 1883.

The first train crossed the new Snake River bridge on April 20, 1884, and

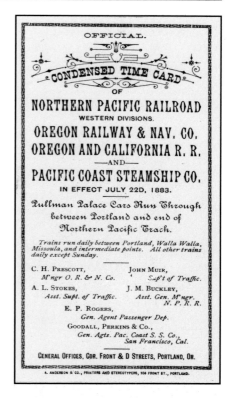

▲ ▲ ▲

In July of 1883 the Northern Pacific Railway express train took just four days to travel from St. Paul, Minnesota, to Portland, Oregon. About 10 trains traveled from San Francisco through Portland to the East each month, and daily service was available between Portland and Ainsworth. Courtesy, Oregon Historical Society

the steamboat *Billings* was transferred to the Cascade division, west of the Columbia. Now that bridge construction was completed, Ainsworth was fading. Some businesses moved out; several others burned.

Work stopped for a while on the line west of the Columbia River but resumed in earnest in the summer, which helped support a boom camp, called Huson, and later helped support the construction of the incline, located in the vicinity of what is now Kennewick. Situated near the shore, the camp consisted of tents used as boarding places and saloons. This area was first called Kennewick in the *Walla Walla Daily Journal* of November 26, 1884: "Considerable excitement in Kennewick—lots going like hotcakes." By the end of 1884, track had been laid past Yakima City (the present Union Gap), about 70 miles west of Kennewick.

In January 1885, the NPRR was reported to have established a new town, Pasco. "It is located in that tropical triangle between the Snake and Columbia, which abounds in sand and lizards, sagebrush and horned toads," the *Walla Walla Union* explained. Most remaining Ainsworth buildings had been moved to Pasco by February; surviving buildings were burned or razed. Ainsworth was discontinued as an NPRR station in March.

The steamboat *Billings* continued as a ferry for trains between Kennewick and Pasco until a bridge was completed in 1888.

During this time, Chinese were an important part of the regional scene, either as railroad employees or miners. Burton Lum, a Kennewick resident, said Chinese mined in the 1880s near the downstream end of Hog Island near Kennewick (now inundated by the reservoir behind McNary Dam). The Chinese wore harnesses to work a treadmill, which pumped water for mining, and Lum saw as many as 50 Chinese yoked together to move a drift log that "resembled a huge centipede." Although their life was menial, Lum described the men as "quite intelligent"; they could read and write their language and work mathematical problems on an abacus. Each mining season, they returned to the island from downriver.

▲ ▲ ▲

The town of Ainsworth pictured here in 1884, was established in 1879 as a railroad construction depot. Newspapers of the day described it as one of the "most uncomfortable, abominable places in America . . . a slice of slums from New York set down in the West." Upon completion in 1883, construction cost of the railroad bridge that spanned the Snake River was more than $1 million—three times greater than the original estimate. Courtesy, Historical Photograph Collections, Washington State University Libraries

▲ ▲ ▲

The steamboat **Frederick K. Billings** *performed many functions during its travels on the Columbia River, which included ferrying train cars (two at a time) between Pasco and Kennewick. The boat is pictured here on July 4, 1890, during a holiday river trip. Courtesy, Oregon Historical Society*

Some Orientals settled in a Pasco "Chinatown" near the railroad tracks. The most prominent of these was Wong How, who established a general store in the late 1880s. He was the father of James Wong Howe, later a famous Hollywood cinematographer who filmed *The Rose Tatoo* (1955), *Hud* (1963), and *Funny Lady* (1975).

Pasco residents hoped their new village could profit from steamboat trade with the upper Columbia River by supplying mines in the Okanogan area, which were attracting attention in the late 1880s. In 1888, two steamboats were constructed at Pasco under the supervision of John Holland to cater to the mine trade. But Priest Rapids was a serious barrier to boats going up the Columbia.

Thomas L. Nixon and Linus Post of Tacoma bought the boats. In 1888 Captain William P. Gray of Pasco managed to take the smallest, the *City of Ellensburgh*, over Priest Rapids. Cargo was carried by wagon from the new NPRR town of Ellensburgh (later spelled Ellensburg) to Port Eaton on the Columbia River and loaded on the steamboat for trips to the Okanogan mining country. In 1892, the other boat, the *Thomas L. Nixon*, was taken over Priest Rapids, and both craft served as cargo and passenger carriers on the upper river in the 1890s.

A final surge of railroad building took place in the early 1900s. The major project was the "North Bank" railroad, so named because much of it was constructed along the north bank of the Columbia below Kennewick and Pasco. When the company was organized in 1905, it was known as the Portland and Seattle Railway, but the name was changed in early 1908 to the Spokane, Portland and Seattle Railway (SP&S).

Times were getting considerably livelier in 1906 because people were arriving daily by railroad, and some undesirable individuals were among the new arrivals. Robberies increased in Kennewick, and on October 31, 1906, a posse

▲ ▲ ▲

A man of many talents and unflagging energy, Captain W.P. Gray pursued a lifelong effort to bring prosperity to the community of Pasco. He served as mayor and land agent for the Northern Pacific Railroad and traveled throughout Washington publicizing and promoting the area. In 1929 the **Pasco Herald** *eulogized Gray as the "embodiment of energy, courage, and vision." Courtesy, Ted Van Arsdol*

The S.N. McGee's Cigar Factory opened on Lewis Street in Pasco in 1907 and put cigars on the market within three weeks. The **Pasco Express** *bragged, "They are selling them as fast as they can turn them out." Prices ranged from 5 cents to 15 cents for the eight brands, which had colorful names such as Jewel, El Vago, El Pasco, and Coupon. Courtesy, Oregon Historical Society*

looking for criminals near town encountered armed suspects. In the ensuing shootout, Marshal Michael Glover was killed, as well as a suspect, deputy sheriff, and one bystander, who was accidentally shot by a posse member. In addition Benton County Sheriff Alexander McNeill was wounded in the shootout. Eventually the posse captured a 16-year-old boy. Several hundred armed men in town prepared for a lynching, but a strong guard was placed at the jail, and the boy later was taken to the county jail at Prosser where he escaped.

Material for the first part of the rail line in the Kennewick and Pasco area was assembled at Ainsworth, and workers began laying track from Kennewick to the south at the start of 1907. A visitor to Pasco in May 1907 reported that the population had increased several times over the 1906 total, and 1,200 laborers were in town, all with jobs. "There is more excitement in town now than in an ordinary place on circus day," the writer informed the *Yakima Herald.* "Everything is booming wonderfully."

SP&S track laying started east from Vancouver, Washington, in September 1907, and after the two groups of track layers met in March 1908, a golden spike was driven near Stevenson, Washington, signifying the completion of the railroad between Pasco and Vancouver. Part of the SP&S line also connected

Pasco and Spokane.

The next entry in the railroad competition was begun by the North Coast Railroad Company, headed by Robert Strahorn, who had purchased the light and power facilities at Kennewick and Pasco in 1908. The North Coast Railroad constructed a bridge on the Columbia just below the Snake in 1910. Track was extended through Kennewick to Benton City, where it crossed the Yakima River. The track was continued to Yakima in 1911. The North Coast was owned by the Oregon Railway and Navigation Company, which changed its name to Oregon-Washington Railway and Navigation Company about this time.

Strahorn was a strong booster of irrigation projects near new railroads. "We must sink or swim by reclamation of some sort almost everywhere," he explained. Strahorn was instrumental in setting up the ill-fated Pasco Reclamation Company near Pasco.

Steamboats were active along the waterfronts during railroad construction days and also carried cargo for several years to the new irrigation towns of Richland, Hanford, and White Bluffs, on the Columbia above Kennewick. The boats were able to travel only six to eight miles per hour when going upriver, depending on the current, said Charles Sanford, office manager of Hanford Irrigation and Power Company. He explained that the advent of a smaller boat, the gas-powered *Hanford Flyer*, provided speedier service for passengers.

A new transcontinental railway, the Chicago, Milwaukee, and St. Paul line, was constructed to the north, crossing the Columbia at Beverly upstream from the Priest Rapids area. In 1912-13, a branch line was extended downriver to serve Hanford and White Bluffs.

By the time of World War I, the great era of railroad construction had ended. Automobiles were gaining rapidly in popularity and the building of many miles of paved roads after the war accelerated the growth of this type of transportation.

▲ ▲ ▲

Pictured in 1926, Robert Strahorn, who appreciated the great resources of the Inland Empire, originated and built the North Coast Railroad. He paid for the construction work, costing millions, with his own personal funds. It was later revealed that North Coast was an extension of the Oregon Railway and Navigation Company. Competition for ownership and control of a profitable railway and prosperous river traffic made it advantageous to conceal that connection. Courtesy, Oregon Historical Society

▲ ▲ ▲

The Hanford Flyer gasoline-powered launch carried passengers and some freight between Kennewick, Hanford, and White Bluffs. The owners of the boat had the U.S. Mail contract in 1908, making two trips each day by 1909. The upriver run ordinarily took three and one half hours, while the downriver trip was usually completed in two hours. Courtesy, Eastern Washington State Historical Society

CHAPTER THREE

Reclaiming the Desert
▲ ▲ ▲

I n earlier years, one of Pasco's promotions involved sending a midget and a very tall man to meet trains at the depot. The small man was said to represent the community, lacking irrigation; the taller individual symbolized the results of water applied to the arid lands.

Pasco and Kennewick area residents lived in expectation of the green farmlands and expanding prosperity resulting from reclamation. Real estate promoters embellished these possibilities in their printed flyers. But most people underestimated the problems to be overcome.

Passing through on trains, passengers saw mostly sagebrush-covered desert, two small towns, and frequently open-range livestock, still roaming, in the 1890s and early 1900s. Many of these animals were horses coming down from

Horse Heaven plateau near Kennewick to drink Columbia River water. "The tramp of their feet was like the roar of thunder," historian W.D. Lyman wrote.

Pasco jumped to an ambitious start, getting the first weekly newspaper, the *Headlight* in 1888, and incorporating in 1891. Editor I.N. Muncy was an enthusiastic promoter who advertised Pasco as "the future great," and its slogan, "Keep Your Eye on Pasco," became well known. After all, the boosters liked to point out, Northern Pacific President Henry Villard had predicted "a great city" would develop in the area where the Snake and Columbia met.

The Pasco Land Company managed to sell numerous town lots to buyers from the Pacific Northwest and other parts of the nation, ending with a flurry of sales in Chicago shortly before the World's Columbian Exposition in 1893.

▲ ▲ ▲

Small rural schoolhouses, like this one in Burbank where barefoot students were photographed by Asahel Curtis in 1909, were the backbone of education in the many small towns of Benton and Franklin counties and adjoining areas. The basic curriculum of reading, writing, and arithmetic, with some geography, was sometimes enlivened by poetry recitations, spelling bees, and singing. Courtesy, Washington State Historical Society

(The exposition celebrated the 400th anniversary of the discovery of America.) But the speculative fever collapsed in the hard times of the 1890s. For Pasco, the decline arrived in late 1892, when "money became as scarce as hen's teeth," W.P. Gray, a Pasco promoter, recalled.

Pasco leaders encouraged plans for irrigation. A major proposal involved bringing Palouse River water through coulees and several small lakes about 60 miles to the Pasco area. Work started on the project in 1893, but only about 10 miles of canal were completed near the Palouse River before financial problems forced a shutdown. The *Headlight* flickered out in 1892, but a little later in the decade the *News* was started, then succeeded by the *News-Recorder*. Both related local events as the town of about 250 people waited for more favorable times.

Located west of the Columbia River, the Yakima Irrigating and Improvement Company (YI&I) was important to the local area in the early 1890s. The company, financed from Oneida, New York, and organized in 1888, completed a short canal from Yakima River to Kiona, 18 miles west of Kennewick. But the YI&I's principal plan was to build a canal to divert water from near Horn Rapids on the Yakima River to Kennewick, then build a canal along the west bank of the Columbia to a point opposite Wallula, more than 30 miles.

Meantime landowners voted in Dell Haven Irrigation District in December

1890. The district apparently agreed to a canal proposal with C.H. Leadbetter, similar to the YI&I project. Leadbetter and his associates, Henry E. Simmons and J.M. Jones, proposed a canal that would start at the Yakima River in the Prosser area, would pass south of Rattlesnake Hills in what is now the Hanford site, and would reach Priest Rapids on the Columbia. The publicity sent many prospective settlers scurrying to the areas near the proposed canals.

Both the YI&I and Dell Haven companies started building toward Kennewick. After some dispute and litigation, the YI&I acquired the Leadbetter interests in 1893. That year the YI&I canal was completed to Kennewick, which by now had built the Hotel Columbia and established a short-lived newspaper, the *Columbian*. In 1893, Leadbetter's Prosser Falls and Priest Rapids Irrigation Company claimed to have finished 25 miles of canal from Prosser Falls (now Prosser), and was looking forward to delivering water in 1894.

Also in 1893, the Sunnyside Canal further up Yakima Valley was completed. All through the valley, irrigation was the hoped-for panacea. However, the U.S. economic situation was increasingly desperate: the stock market collapsed, banks suspended operations, and numerous businesses failed. One result of local economic problems was the transfer of the Kennewick canal from the YI&I Company to Dell Haven Irrigation District in 1893. On the

▲ ▲ ▲

The Northern Pacific railroad bridge crossed the Yakima River near Kiona, close to this U.S. Geological Survey Gauging Station waterwheel. Wooden waterwheels were used to lift water from the river to flumes, which then carried the water to the fields. The unidentified gentleman in this late 1890s photograph holds a baby on his knee. Courtesy, U.S. Bureau of Reclamation

▲ ▲ ▲

ABOVE: The roundhouse in Pasco expanded from four stalls in 1888 to 38 stalls at its completion. By 1906 the Northern Pacific had built 26 miles of track in their terminal yard where more than 250 men were employed. Since Pasco was the lowest point on the railroad in eastern Washington the trains were able to take advantage of the down-hill grade by using fewer engines. Courtesy, Eastern Washington State Historical Society

FACING PAGE, TOP: A gentleman waits patiently for the stage on the main street of Kahlotus around 1907. Businesses common to most small towns in the early twentieth century included a grocery store, livery stable, post office, drug store, cigar and candy store, and a men's clothing store. Courtesy, Eastern Washington State Historical Society

Leadbetter (Prosser Falls) project, the Yakima County sheriff confiscated the company possessions to pay debts.

Writing in 1896 from Kennewick, I.W. Dudley of the YI&I Company still expressed a view that the project was the state's best bet for irrigation, but he did not know how long the financial "drain" and "risk" could be permitted to continue. "Many of our wealthiest men in the state today are worse off than nothing and completely broken and bankrupt," he wrote.

Land in Kennewick's vicinity had turned green in the mid-1890s when canal water was applied, but maintenance problems developed, and in several seasons much of the property reverted to its brown and wasted natural state.

In the 1890s, the Walla Walla River above Wallula also was the focus of irrigation experiments. Ditches west of Walla Walla provided water for gardens and orchards. One ditch from Mill Creek, a Walla Walla River tributary, was proposed for extension to Wallula but seems to have encountered financial obstacles. Buckets attached to water wheels scooped out water from the lower river for some farmers.

When better times arrived about the turn of the century, the most logical project for an early revival was at Kennewick, where so much work had been completed. Frank Dudley, head of the YI&I Company, retained part of his lands but sold his lower tract to J.P. Morgan & Company, and this was taken over by a Northern Pacific land company. The few remaining voters of Dell Haven Irrigation District balloted to dissolve their organization, and Northwestern Improvement Company bought the Kennewick ditch and property at a public auction in 1901.

In 1902, Northwestern Improvement Company conveyed its land in the Kennewick area to Northern Pacific Irrigation Company. Charles S. Mellen, NPRR president, headed both firms. Town lots went on sale in 1902, the ditch was repaired, and in 1903 the first water arrived at Kennewick. Sales through the Kennewick Land Company were brisk, and the new town was incorporated and flourished.

Many dryland-farm homesteaders also moved into the areas near Kennewick and Pasco about this time.

In 1906 a large influx of new residents at Pasco was spurred by prospects of railroad construction. Yet many of the town's hopes still were pinned on potential irrigation. The U.S. Bureau of Reclamation had been studying the possibility of the federal government taking on the old plan of bringing water to Pasco from Palouse River, but rejected the idea, strangling the project "in its infancy," as the *Pasco Express* reported. "Had it been a bastard its treatment

could not have been worse," the editor lamented in 1906.

C.B. Cox, a young government engineer on the Palouse project, noticed that many settlers had staked out claims and built shacks near the route of the proposed canal.

"The crew was moving out," Cox remembered. "We were at Eltopia on a train headed for Yakima. It was quite a little town then. I was on the back platform and there was quite a crowd of farmers. They knew me and picked up rocks and heaved 'em at me. They were sore—sore as a boil. Oh, how they cussed."

These settlers knew their chances were slim without water. Although dryland wheat farming was tried and much was grown, many discouraged farmers moved away in the next few years. This was in sharp contrast with an irrigated area such as Kennewick, where strawberries were an important early crop. Orchards and vineyards also had begun flourishing on the river banks.

Between the Snake River and Wallula, irrigation companies were attempting to develop farms and townsites along the Columbia's east bank. One promoter who diverted water from the Snake River to land near present-day Burbank was declared insolvent as early as 1906, and another organization took over the project. In 1906 another enterprise, the Columbia Canal, was said to be ready to reclaim 10,000 acres along the Columbia River. This project brought water from a few miles up the Walla Walla River.

A new town, Attalia, sprang up north of Wallula, and struggled for a number of years. One ex-resident commented much

▲ ▲ ▲

BELOW: Customers could receive a shave, haircut, or shoeshine at Joe Martin's barbershop on Kennewick Avenue near Washington Street in downtown Kennewick around the turn of the century. Martin is pictured here standing behind the rear chair. Courtesy, East Benton County Historical Society

▲ ▲ ▲

Pacific Power and Light and the Pasco Electric companies offered premiums and specials in the Pasco Herald *as more and more home-owners wired their houses for the modern convenience of electricity. A 1919 advertisement for the Pasco Electric Company boasted "some of the swellest light fixtures you ever saw. A whole dray load . . . you just must see them; they are great." Courtesy, Oregon Historical Society*

later about that town's survival problems: "If all the tears shed over Attalia could have been used for irrigation, the project could have been saved."

Near the mouth of the Yakima River, W.R. and Howard Amon bought property in 1904 at what is now Richland, from Ben and Mary Rosencrance, who had raised livestock and irrigated their farm by using a big waterwheel that pulled water from the river. In 1905 the Amons purchased the Nelson Rich farm on the lower river as well as Rich's canal. That same year, Howard Amon's Benton Water Company extended a six-mile canal from the Yakima River to a new town on the old Rosencrance farm called Benton, soon renamed Richland.

A canal extension to irrigate land north of Richland was completed in 1909, and in 1910 the town was incorporated.

Further north, in the area below Priest Rapids, water wheels and pumps had been used to irrigate lands near the Columbia. E.W. Craig, postmaster at Julia, more than 40 miles upstream from Kennewick, operated one wheel, which watered 25 acres. Julia was near an old freighting road that left the east bank and went toward the mining regions. Craig was probably looking forward to the possibilities of a canal from Priest Rapids, a proposal discussed since the 1890s.

Julia, however, was upstaged by the establishment of two other communities, Hanford and White Bluffs, in 1907. Hanford Irrigation and Power Company began construction of a canal, and in 1908 a power plant was completed at Priest Rapids. Power generated at Priest Rapids was transmitted 15 miles east to a pumping plant at Coyote Rapids, where water was pumped into the 18-mile main canal. Some concrete lining was installed before the first reliable supply of water from the canal was available, in 1909, to the Hanford and

White Bluffs areas.

Hanford was named after Judge C.H. Hanford of Seattle, an official of the Hanford Irrigation and Power Company. For a little while the post office was named Fordnah, because another Hanford community and post office existed in the state; the first Hanford post office closed a short time later.

The Hanford irrigation company planned to build another canal at a higher elevation than the first one, and there was talk of reclaiming 300,000 acres eventually. Other smaller projects in the area were operated by gas and electric plants.

In 1910, work started on a major reclamation project called Wahluke, located on the Columbia's north bank below White Bluffs. This same year brought new entries into the power business in the Tri-Cities area. Pacific Power & Light Company (PP&L) was organized in this year, and among its plants in central Washington were water works and electric plants at Pasco and Kennewick. The company

▲ ▲ ▲

ABOVE: As efforts were made to ready the land for farming and irrigation, E.V. Smalley described the basic method of clearing sagebrush in a February 12, 1894, article in **The Northwest Magazine.** *". . . hitch a team to a chain, throw the chain around each shrub and jerk it out by the roots. The larger shrubs have a valve for fuel. The others are piled up and burned. All the settlers use sagebrush for their home fires." Courtesy, Washington State Historical Society*

▲ ▲ ▲

LEFT: Spare parts lined the riverbank close to this 1909 powerhouse on the Snake River near Pasco. Irrigation water entered the pumphouse from a reservoir and was delivered to the fields through a pipe built of wooden staves. Courtesy, Washington State Historical Society

▲ ▲ ▲

Water from the Columbia Irrigation Canal enabled the establishment of orchards in "The Highlands" in 1908. The promise that trees would bear fruit just six years after planting created a population boom in the area. Fruit was marketed through regional growers associations. For a time, the Northern Pacific held a fruit distribution contract that controlled 60 percent of the crops in Oregon, Washington, and Montana. Courtesy, East Benton County Historical Society

reported that pumping for irrigation would take place on the Columbia between Pasco and Beverly, in addition to activity at Yakima and Walla Walla, and PP&L was ready to supply the power. The PP&L extended one electrical line from Kennewick to tie in with the Priest Rapids and Coyote Rapids line, and considerable irrigation took place from wells in the Hanford and White Bluffs vicinity, starting in 1911.

Also in 1910, American Power & Light Co. bought the Hanford Irrigation and Power Company, which lacked financing for needed improvements.

Because of the reclamation projects in the area, times seemed good at Hanford and White Bluffs. Wealth and prosperity were reflected in names such as El Dorado Orchard Tracts and Klondike Terrace Point Orchards, typical sagebrush property for sale. But buyers had to dig their own wells, then hook up the electricity needed to pump water to the crops.

Near Pasco, a prominent Seattle developer, James A. Moore, completed a mansion, and then began irrigating fruit trees by pumping water from the Columbia with a gas engine. Five- and ten-acre tracts in Moore's "fruit land and garden tracts" near his home went on sale in 1909.

The Pasco Reclamation Company completed a pumping plant two miles above the mouth of the Snake River, and moved ahead in 1909 with plans to irrigate more than 10,000 acres encircling much of Pasco.

Across the Columbia, Northern Pacific Irrigation Company announced it would irrigate 3,500 acres on the Highlands just west of Kennewick. According to the company, machinery was to be installed that was capable of lifting 12 million gallons of water from the Columbia every 24 hours. Northwestern Light and Power Company was installing a large substation to provide power and also was building a pumping station for domestic water. A booster pamphlet hailed the Highlands as "an ideal location for fruit growers and home builders."

In those times, said long-time Kennewick resident Jay Perry, there was "a common belief that if a person owned 10 acres of bearing orchard, it would make them a good living."

Strawberry acreage steadily increased, but alfalfa and grapes were among other popular choices for crops. Grape production did so well that Kennewick began staging an annual Grape Festival. The farmers also supplemented their main crops by raising peaches, poultry, and hogs.

The first decade of the new century was a major boon for the area. Census figures for 1910 showed Pasco with 2,083 residents, compared to a population of 254 in 1900, and Kennewick had 1,219 residents, a significant increase from a population of 183 in 1900. Richland's 1910 population was 420, White Bluffs' was 375, Hanford's was 285, Attalia's was 320, and Hover's, below Kennewick,

was 275. Among Franklin County's small dryland-farming towns, Connell led the population count with 500.

In contrast with the prosperous beginnings of 1900-1910, the next decade brought sobering events and an awareness of the limitations of the irrigation entrepreneurs. In several other western states, a similar transition was under way; investors were shying away from irrigation in the years just before World War I.

In numerous instances, promoters did not want to be burdened with maintenance of irrigation facilities after making quick profits from land sales. Other problems involved inferior construction, water shortage, mismanagement, and fraud. Settlers also ran into difficulties marketing crops and financing their farms.

The most shocking news of 1912 was the financial collapse of the Wahluke project. Companies backing this venture had sold $5 million worth of bonds, yet by 1912 the bonds were declared in news stories as "entirely worthless." All Wahluke promoters who could be found were being arrested.

In 1911, the PP&L proposed to construct a hydroelectric dam costing

▲ ▲ ▲

In the early days of Kennewick High School, a graduating class of 10 students was considered large. The athletic teams rose to the challenge of maintaining enough students, as illustrated by this 1909 girls basketball team, coached by Lynn Shanafelt (far right). The team included Nellie Hoadley, Effie Oliver, Jessie Perry, Georgia Staley, Jessie Folsom, and Bernice Griffith. Courtesy, East Benton County Historical Society

▲ ▲ ▲

Co-operative Extension information about insects, crops, and diseases played an important role in the development of agriculture in the Columbia Basin. In 1916 these 4-H members, leaders, and officials from Washington State College gathered at agriculturist Lee Lampson's home with 4-H projects at their feet. This house was one of the first homes constructed in Kennewick Highlands. Courtesy, East Benton County Historical Society

$5 million to $10 million at Priest Rapids. But the Hanford Irrigation and Power Company declared bankruptcy in early 1913, which seemed to cast a shadow over additional planning for that area. A federal judge set up a receivership to carry out the company's obligations to stockholders.

At Pasco, failure of the Pasco Reclamation Company hurt the community. In a suit filed in 1911, the Bank of Pasco said property in the town "has been greatly depreciated in value" because of the company's problems. A 1914 report listed the company pipes as rotting and unable to provide water, and termed the company insolvent.

Residents were forced to take over more responsibility for operating and maintaining the canals, and did so through irrigation districts. In 1917, the Franklin County Irrigation District was established, serving an area west of Pasco from a pumping plant on the Columbia. And in 1917, Northern Pacific Irrigation Company sold its system at Kennewick to the new Columbia Irrigation District.

Assets of the Hanford Irrigation and Power Company were put on sale in 1915. The winning bidder represented Henry K.T. Lyons of Denver, Colorado, who turned the property over to Black Rock Power and Irrigation Company. The Consumers Ditch Company and Agathon Land Company also were active. One probable reason for continuing interest of the power companies in this area was that they wanted to retain the power rights for nearby Priest Rapids, which went with the power and irrigation facilities already completed.

Individual farmers still were not making big gains; a soil survey in the White Bluffs area in 1916 concluded that in some cases, the cost of water was prohibitive when balanced against probable crop prices.

World War I brought a temporary distraction from irrigation and reclamation problems. Many young men left for military service, and people at home bought Liberty Bonds as well as observed meatless and wheatless days to conserve food. Meanwhile a temporary rise in food prices aided the area's farmers.

The towns welcomed the end of World War I, on November 11, 1918. Syble Lagerquist, a Pasco resident at the time, recalled:

Impromptu parades formed on the outskirts and surged toward the center of town. Steam locomotives blew their whistles. The crowd came in like the tentacles of an octopus curling towards its center. They merged at the beautiful Liberty Theater for memorial services, and gave thanks to God. There was dancing in the street that night . . .

On the dryland-farming front, a series of extra dry seasons led to more agricultural failures among homesteaders. Years of greater-than-average precipitation, in what is now the Columbia Basin Project, were followed by dry years from 1917 to 1922; summers were almost rainless. "The result was an abandonment of considerable areas, in some cases practically whole townships being permitted to return to a dry state," a 1928 report mentioned. Survivors were "fighting a hard battle" in their efforts to grow wheat. A series of bank failures took place about this same time.

A more positive development in the area—and statewide—was improved transportation; auto ownership increased rapidly, and roads were improved. One highlight of 1916 was the establishment of a bus line between Kennewick and White Bluffs. The rivers, however, were a barrier to overland transportation expansion. Only ferries, which thrived for a while, were available to carry large amounts of traffic across the rivers.

▲ ▲ ▲

The 1920s and 1930s saw the introduction of tractors used during the harvest season. Spark arresters were placed over the smokestacks of the tractors to prevent the ripe grain from catching fire. Here, a harvest crew poses with a tractor, a wagon piled with wheat, and a stationary belt-driven threshing machine. Courtesy, East Benton County Historical Society

▲ ▲ ▲

Ferries, like this one pictured here in 1920, ran from Burbank to Pasco on the Snake River, and crossed back and forth on the Snake and Columbia rivers; passengers yelled for the boat if they were on the opposite shore. More than one automobile was lost to the river when passengers were in a hurry or when car brakes were inadequate. Courtesy, East Benton County Historical Society

▲ ▲ ▲

Calculated to hold a 42-ton load, the planked Columbia River Toll Bridge was 3,300 feet in length and 20 feet wide. The tollhouse was located on the Pasco side, and receipts on opening weekend in October 1921 totaled nearly $550. Monthly passes were available until the tolls were removed on July 1, 1931. Courtesy, Franklin County Historical Society

Bridging the Snake and Columbia rivers became imperative as local and long-distance traffic increased. The first highway bridge spanned the Snake River a short distance above the old Northern Pacific railroad bridge at Ainsworth. Washington Governor Louis Hart was the featured speaker at the dedication on May 5, 1921, attended by what was said to be the largest crowd ever gathered in one place in the area.

On October 21, 1922, a Columbia River bridge connecting Kennewick and Pasco was dedicated. At the time, the highway was part of "the Yellowstone Trail." Tolls were collected on the Snake River bridge until 1927 and on the Columbia River bridge until 1931.

In the early 1920s, Pasco and Franklin County took the lead in the new field of air transportation. The Pasco Chamber of Commerce pushed for an airfield, and by 1926 the city had acquired land east of the Northern Pacific tracks and southeast of the city cemetery for the facility. County commissioners provided funds for a hangar and other air field improvements.

A crowd estimated at 2,500 was present for the first airmail flight from Pasco to Elko, Nevada, via Boise, Idaho, on April 6, 1926. Old-time stage driver Felix Warren even brought some Spokane mail by stagecoach to the new airfield for the first flight by pilot Leon Cuddeback. A case of Kennewick grape juice for President Calvin Coolidge was included in the cargo before takeoff time.

But the airplane business was small-scale in the 1920s. Many people still traveled by rail, and Pasco's position of being the largest town in the area was bolstered by its roundhouse and large railroad payroll.

Neighboring Kennewick envisioned some gain in its stature by wresting the Benton county seat from Prosser, at the western end of the county. Kennewick had obtained an injunction in 1916 against construction of a permanent courthouse at Prosser. But an election in 1926 on the courthouse issue gave Prosser a two-thirds majority, and immediately afterward, bonds were issued to build a permanent courthouse there.

At Richland, residents had taken over the irrigation system about 1920, through the Richland Irrigation District. The population remained small in the 1920s, between 200 and 300 residents. A Richland sign of the 1920s pointed the way to "the Hanford oil fields" in Rattlesnake Hills. Drilling for gas and oil had started there a few years earlier, and gas from the wells eventually served several Yakima Valley towns. Drilling at Attalia about the same time failed to turn up any significant oil, despite much publicity.

In the early 1920s, Washington state intervened in the White Bluffs irrigation project by setting up a "land settlement" plan for World War I veterans and others. The plan divided the land into one hundred 20-acre tracts, which included wells. But numerous complaints about operating costs and the inability of farmers to earn a sufficient profit resulted in the state dropping out in 1926. The state sold unsettled or foreclosed tracts, and gave refunds or reached other settlements with people still on the land.

Washington Irrigation and Development Company (WID), a subsidiary of General Electric Company, received a franchise from the U.S. Congress in 1925 to develop the power at Priest Rapids. This hydroelectric development was expected to bring industrial plants to the area, which would irrigate 100,000 acres and would provide for a city of 40,000 to 50,000 people. The WID proposal was not carried to completion, but Priest Rapids Dam was built later by the Grant County Public Utility District; construction started in 1956 and the first power was generated in 1959.

In the 1920s, Pasco leaders considered a "Five-Mile" project on the Snake River as a good way to obtain electrical power and water pumping capability for irrigation. A dam at Five-Mile Rapids—a short distance below the present-day Ice Harbor Dam—had been considered for a long time, and would have been especially timely to aid Burbank, a small irrigation project on the south side of the Snake that obtained its water from that river.

A small "wing dam" in the Five-Mile vicinity was renovated in the mid-1920s. The dam was supposed to provide sufficient water so that the

▲ ▲ ▲

Aviator Leon Cuddeback carried some 200 pounds of mail in a Swallow biplane, initiating Varney Airline's airmail service with a flight to Elko, Nevada. The mail was ceremoniously delivered by 73-year-old Felix Warren, who drove a stagecoach from Spokane, picked up the mail at the Pasco post office, and brought it to the airport. The airport was located south of the cemetery in East Pasco at that time. Courtesy, United Air Lines

▲ ▲ ▲

The well-stocked NP Grocery on Lewis Street near First Avenue supplied Pasco citizens with groceries, fish, and notions, including grass seed, in the 1920s. Owner Harry Yamauchi (right) was assisted by (from left to right) Shizue Sumida and two of his daughters, Chiyoko and Haruye Yamauchi. If customers lacked cash they could trade livestock and household goods for staples. Courtesy, Oregon Historical Society

hydraulic system at Burbank could keep the canal from Snake River to Burbank supplied all season. But the project was near its end in the late 1920s; lack of financing was an important factor.

Attalia, another irrigation project, a short distance upstream on the Columbia from Wallula, also was dying. A.C. Amon, who started and operated the Farmers Exchange in Kennewick in 1923, said he bought cattle from Attalia residents "going broke" and shipped a carload each month to Seattle. Bernice Cummings, Wallula historian, said the Attalia project had practically died out by 1930. She cited lack of water and expense of operation as reasons for the failure of the project.

In the early 1930s, asparagus was becoming a popular crop in the Kennewick area. Many fruit trees were removed to make way for vegetables. A 1931 directory credited Kennewick with several hotels, two auto camps, a port commission, the Kennewick Valley Telephone Company, and a variety of other businesses.

Further north, the Priest Rapids irrigation and canal system was sold in 1931 to its customers. The system was transferred after considerable litigation and disputes had been resolved, which extended back several years, pitting farmers against the company owners. The sale was one final reminder that irrigation had not been a profit-making venture for private firms.

The 1920s had been difficult for the farmers, but the 1930s brought even more problems, as a nationwide Depression developed. Unemployment was running high, and many homeless persons were riding freight trains through the area.

Pasco received a blow to its transportation role in 1933 when United Airlines announced it was relocating its air passenger and freight services from Pasco to Pendleton, Oregon. United was the successor to Varney Airlines and three other airlines that merged in 1931. The Pasco airfield, which had been relocated in 1929 to a site near the present Tri-Cities Airport, received only intermittent use in the 1930s, following the departure of United Airlines. The move left the local communities feeling isolated.

Irrigation and reclamation again became the focus of local residents during the Franklin D. Roosevelt administration starting in 1933, when the federal government decided to become actively involved with Columbia River hydroelectric projects. As a result of that decision, building of the Grand Coulee Dam was approved and construction began in 1934 in northeast Washington. Eventually water would be pumped out of a reservoir behind the dam and

▲ ▲ ▲

The early 1920s brought prosperity and a traffic light to Kennewick. Here, Model-T cars, trucks, and businesses line what is now Kennewick Avenue. Other signs of progress include Piggly Wiggly, the first clerkless grocery, which opened in May 1926; a growing number of garages and service stations with curbside gasoline pumps like the one seen on the right; and The Evelyn Shoppe, a beauty parlor owned by Evelyn Serier, who brought the first permanent wave machine to the area. Courtesy, Ted Van Arsdol

▲ ▲ ▲

Men trimmed the ends after women sorted and stacked asparagus spears at long tables in this Kennewick packing shed during the early 1930s. The man with the large knife appears to be cutting the tips of especially small spears. Courtesy, Washington State Historical Society

brought through canals and coulees to the "Big Bend" country and as far south as Pasco. This was a much more ambitious reclamation project than the Palouse plan, which had been rejected by the federal government in the early 1900s.

But successful government efforts, such as the Yakima Project in the upper Yakima Valley in the early 1900s, had shown that such major undertakings could achieve results. The first consideration, though, at the Grand Coulee Dam was power, and a timetable on the delivery of water as far south as the Snake River was somewhat vague in the 1930s.

A proposed hydroelectric project near Umatilla, Oregon, which eventually was named in honor of Senator Charles McNary of Oregon, received widespread support and publicity from Pacific Northwest leaders in the 1930s. The first actual step in dam and navigation lock building on the lower Columbia River was Bonneville Dam, completed in 1937. The Bonneville drowned the rapids at the Cascades, permitting barge traffic to travel from the lower to upper Columbia River, in addition to supplying much needed power to the region.

Kennewick and Pasco area residents were enthused about the possibilities of river traffic and the benefits it could bring. Residents welcomed the tug *Mary Gail*, which traveled upriver in 1937 and in 1940 welcomed the tug *M. V. Keith*, which passed upriver from Portland to Lewiston. The Port of Pasco was organized in 1940 to accommodate increased river traffic. In 1941, two 175-foot barges were launched at Kennewick. One was christened the *Port of Kennewick*, while the other, built for Walla Walla Grain Growers, Inc., was christened at Port Kelley on the Columbia River below Wallula.

But river commerce in 1940-1941 was more of a potential than actual fact. And the towns near the Snake and Columbia junction remained tiny compared to the Northwest's thriving cities. Although Pasco had gained in population— up from 3,362 in 1920 to 3,496 in 1930 and 3,913 in 1940—the population gain was less than 600 in 20 years. Kennewick's total population was 1,918 in 1940, up slightly from 1,519 in 1930 and 1,684 in 1920.

At this time, the Tri-Cities name had not come into use yet. Sometimes Kennewick and Pasco were referred to as the Twin Cities, and the area was

mentioned in occasional railroad publicity as Three Rivers.

Editor Hill Williams of the *Pasco Herald* wrote in 1941 that one chance after another had been "doomed to failure" for Pasco, and old timers had "grown a little skeptical." He hoped the area was not facing more disappointments, as the nation moved out of the Depression into a new era.

Then a jarring event changed history's course, affecting even the small communities of the Tri-Cities. On December 7, 1941, Japanese airplanes attacked Pearl Harbor, and the United States entered World War II. Area residents braced for the probability that many sons would join the armed forces for the global conflict.

As the country mobilized, government and military officials were considering what new installations needed to be developed to aid the war effort.

What had not been much of an asset so far in some parts of central Washington—a lot of wide open, isolated space—soon became a real benefit from the military standpoint. Here was room for airfields and other training facilities, and the dry, clear climate provided many good flying days. Dispersal of new military facilities to remote inland areas must have seemed especially beneficial in the months after the Pearl Harbor attack, when many persons were nervous about possible Japanese attacks along the Pacific Coast.

▲ ▲ ▲

Long distances, open spaces, and sunny skies made flying an ideal hobby for mid-Columbia citizens in the 1930s. These aviatrixes posed together in flight suits near a monoplane on the Fourth of July in 1935. Gladys Vicker Crook, shown driving the tractor, flew in area stunt shows. Her husband, Edward Crook, had a flying school and managed the Pasco Airport from 1936 to 1937. Courtesy, East Benton County Historical Society

CHAPTER FOUR

Hanford
And
Manhattan
▲ ▲ ▲

I n January 1942, the month after the Japanese attack on Pearl Harbor, navy Lieutenant Commander B.B. Smith arrived in Pasco to acquire land for a naval air station. Smith, commanding the Reserve Aviation Base at Sandpoint Naval Air Station in Seattle, was impressed with the year-round flying weather in Pasco and the availability of cheap land. By March, machines were grading and smoothing land, and work had started on barracks and other base facilities.

Residents were surprised and often amazed at the onrush of wartime activity that climaxed with construction and operation of a plutonium production plant in Benton County. Many thousands of newcomers arrived to help build and man the naval air station, army transportation facilities, and the Hanford Engineer

▲ ▲ ▲
Some 3,000 people attended the dedication of the new Columbia River bridge on July 30, 1954. Chairman of the Roads and Bridges Committee of the Washington State Legislature, Julia Butler Hansen (center), was joined by Miss Benton County, Betty Sue Hill (left), and Benton County Fair Rodeo Queen, Jean Mullineaux (right), for the ribbon-cutting ceremony. An excited group of children on bicycles were the first to cross the bridge. Courtesy, Ralph Smith

Works; the Tri-Cities economy and atmosphere were transformed permanently.

The U.S. Army planned an Advance General Depot for Pasco in 1942, but abandoned this in April after constructing only 2 of 42 proposed warehouses north of town, close to the railroad yard.

In early 1942, the army started construction of the Pasco Holding and Reconsignment Point (H&R), to be operated by the Transportation Corps on the Columbia River southeast of Pasco. Eight huge warehouses and a complex of railroad tracks were among major features of the depot, which became known as "Big Pasco." The initial warehouses built earlier near the railroad yard were used later as temporary quarters for atomic plant workers and were called "Little Pasco."

Trucks, railroad flatcars, chemicals, flour, surgical equipment, and even gold braid were among the huge amounts of material that was shipped by rail to West Coast ports to be used by U.S. forces and their allies. Transit storage en route was considered vital in controlling rail movements because ports were congested with wartime freight. Before World War II was over, Pasco's H&R Point would process great quantities of lend-lease cargo, much of it bound for the Soviet Union.

Federal officials estimated that a military population of 5,000 would require housing in Pasco, including families of servicemen assigned to the air station. In addition, civilian workers needed places to stay. Kennewick and Pasco residents rented all available rooms, and even garages and autos were used. Small housing projects were constructed in Pasco and Kennewick, but the towns still were crowded beyond capacity. Many newcomers hauled in trailers and set up housekeeping in the makeshift camps.

Naval recruits also arrived for training, and residents got accustomed to seeing small planes in the skies, practicing landings, takeoffs, and other maneuvers. Additional land in Benton and Franklin counties was taken over during the war for use in training; some was used by pilot trainees to practice bombing.

In December 1942, three visitors representing the Corps of Engineers' Manhattan District arrived. The visitors were seeking a site for a top-secret plutonium plant and included Lieutenant Colonel Franklin T. Matthias, Gilbert Church, and Al Hall. The latter two were employees of E.I. du Pont de Nemours & Co., Inc., which had been picked as the primary contractor for the upcoming Hanford atomic project, later called the Manhattan Project.

▲ ▲ ▲

While stationed at the Pasco Naval Air Station, aviation cadets received 84 hours of flying time, including solo aerobatics, formation, and night flying. Pasco was the first naval station to house WAVES on base, and by filling positions as clerks, typists, and mechanics, the women took on responsibilities that increased the number of sailors available for overseas duty. Courtesy, Ralph Smith

We selected the site with only a general idea of the structures required," Matthias wrote. "How many reactors and how many separations buildings was an open question. We tentatively laid out six reactor sites in our preliminary site study, and the three reactors originally built were located almost exactly in three of these locations. Speed and security were the watchwords.

Matthias further explained that the site met requirements listed by Brigadier General Leslie R. Groves, Manhattan District commanding officer. Groves wanted an unpopulated or lightly populated area of 500 to 600 square miles, close to clean water, 25 miles or more from any large city, at least 15 miles

or more from a main-line highway or railroad, and not less than about 200 miles from the coast.

Removal of residents from the irrigated tracts of Hanford, White Bluffs, and Richland was a government priority. Unfortunately, this came at a time when prospects seemed upbeat for the farmers. The irrigation system at White Bluffs and Hanford had been rehabilitated, and crop prices were rising following the Depression.

Richland Postmaster Ed Peddicord recalled that on March 4, 1943, registered letters from the Corps of Engineers were delivered to 1,200 landowners at Hanford, White Bluffs, and Richland, informing them that the U.S. government had condemned their property as of February 23. Residents were given 30 days to move out.

Because of government secrecy, residents were unable to learn the reason for the planned project, except that it was connected with the war. After some mass meetings and protests, the residents complied with the condemnation orders, although many had difficulty finding housing in the nearby area. A large number chose to contest the appraised prices set on their property. Peddicord said "plenty of ill feeling" existed among older residents toward anyone connected with the new project.

Hanford Engineer Works construction started in early 1943. The government quickly built a giant camp at the old irrigation town of Hanford for its construction workers. This community, containing barracks, mess halls, and other facilities, eventually reached a peak population of 51,000—13,000 of these were in a trailer camp. The engineers and Du Pont stressed good food and a varied recreational program to try to keep workers on the project, who were frequently frustrated by the secrecy, isolation, wind, and dust.

▲ ▲ ▲

During the early days of the Hanford Engineer Works the design engineers were only days ahead of the builders. No one knew exactly how plutonium production would proceed, so the structures were heavily reinforced with steel and concrete. Original plans called for four 800-foot-long concrete separation buildings, but only two of the three built were used. Courtesy, Hanford Science Center

▲ ▲ ▲

The construction camp barracks at Hanford housed some 30,000 workers when this photograph was taken in the mid-1940s. About 5,000 of these workers were single women whose barracks were enclosed behind a six-foot-high fence—complete with a guarded entrance. The majestic White Bluffs are seen across the Columbia River. Courtesy, Hanford Science Center

In the nearby area, workers began constructing unusual and often huge structures, which eventually became three reactors, chemical separations buildings, fuel fabrication facilities, and waste storage tanks. Workers were advised not to speculate about the project, but many surmised that some type of super explosive must be involved. This seemed likely, judging from Du Pont's role, and from the buildings' thick walls, which some thought were intended to protect against explosions.

Hanford officials contacted newspaper editors and radio stations in the region, and asked them not to publicize the project. The media cooperated with the request, but some information still slipped through. The *Saturday Evening Post* mentioned that "the biggest war factory in the West" was under construction near Pasco. Dr. Glenn Seaborg, who visited Hanford as a young chemist and saw "a swarm of activity," said officials called the plant "Site W." Noted scientists stopping at Hanford used aliases; one such visitor, Enrico Fermi, solved a reactor problem that threatened Hanford production.

In 1943, the government started construction of a new Richland at the old town of the same name to house 17,000 persons—operators of the plant and their families.

"There was a pervading other-worldness about the area," said Richland resident Margaret Bjorklund.

It wasn't a town in the usual sense of the word . . . All of us were government employees in one sense or another. All of us were tied to the highly restricted area known as the Hanford Works . . . All of us conducted our lives in lookalike buildings all standing in rows. All of these buildings contained strangers who moved here from all over the United States, some of whom "talked funny."

Richland's population "knew no bounds, nor any stability," said teacher

Maevis Hughes. "Boys and girls came and went like bees on a honey tree. Some were extremely bright and well trained, the sons and daughters of many scientists and other professionals the project employed, while many others were scarcely able to read or write."

Richland was entirely government owned and controlled; the government even operated the municipal facilities.

Federal Prison Industries was asked to move in, bringing prisoners to harvest the crops at orchards and vineyards that were taken over in the Hanford area. The prisoners, including some conscientious objectors to the war effort, arrived in early 1944, and were housed in Columbia Camp at Horn Rapids on the Yakima River west of Richland. The harvest continued for several years after the war, with private operators replacing the prisoners in later years.

▲ ▲ ▲

An astounding 25 million meals were served in eight mess halls during the Hanford construction period. About 50 to 60 tons of food were prepared for each meal, and since food seemed unlimited, construction workers would often stuff chicken, chops, and rolls into their overall pockets to take back to the barracks for late night snacks. Courtesy, Robley L. Johnson

▲ ▲ ▲

Every Friday was payday at the Hanford construction site. About $40,000 to $50,000 in money orders would be sold at the post office each week where there were five windows to service the crowd. Workers also stood in line at the Western Union office to send money home to their families. Courtesy, Robley L. Johnson

▲ ▲ ▲

ABOVE: E.I. du Pont was the prime contractor for both the housing and the plant construction of the Hanford works. Some 4,000 homes were built between April 1943 and the end of 1945. In 1946 the monthly rent for a one-bedroom prefab house, including utilities, was $27.50, while a four-bedroom house rented for $67.50 each month. Courtesy, Hanford Science Center

▲ ▲ ▲

FACING PAGE, TOP: The new houses in Richland came supplied with coal, water, wood, electricity, and even a lawn mower. The government maintenance department would paint houses in a buff tone or supply seven different pastel shades if the resident preferred to paint their own house in a different color. By 1949 tenants were asked to assume minor home maintenance tasks, such as replacing fuses, faucet washers, and broken windows. Courtesy, Robley L. Johnson

At the Hanford reservation, plutonium production started late in 1944. Construction tapered off, and in February 1945 the Hanford camp closed because housing no longer was required for construction workers.

Pasco, the first stop for most Hanford workers because of its train facilities, still was a busy place in 1945. Since 1941 the town had more than doubled in population; it now totaled about 10,000 residents. Mayor E.S. Johnston said his job had been comprised of "light civic duty" before the war, but afterwards he had faced many demands such as finding rooms for newcomers, building houses, opening restaurants, and digging water lines.

Hanford plutonium, delivered to Los Alamos, New Mexico, was used in the first atomic explosion at Alamogordo on July 16, 1945. The government's secret finally emerged in the glare of worldwide publicity in August 1945, when the Japanese cities of Nagasaki and Hiroshima were bombed. The public then learned that Hanford had been part of a secret weapons complex, also consisting of facilities at Los Alamos and Oak Ridge, Tennessee. Plutonium for the nuclear device, called "Fat Man," that was used at Nagasaki had come from Hanford. Concentrated uranium from Oak Ridge provided the force for the Hiroshima atomic bomb.

Pasco Naval Air Station was shut down shortly after the war. The H&R Point (also known as Pasco Engineer Depot) acted as a distribution center for vehicles and other surplus military equipment, and in 1947 the War Assets Administration turned over the facility to the Corps of Engineers, Washington National Guard, and other agencies.

At Hanford, General Electric Company (GE) took over from Du Pont as the primary contractor in late 1946, and the Atomic Energy Commission replaced the Corps of Engineers on January 1, 1947, as supervisor of the Hanford facility for the U.S. government. The Cold War with the Soviet Union was under way, and there was much talk of atomic spies and Russian progress on an atomic bomb. Speculation ended when President Harry Truman announced in 1949 that the Communists had exploded an atomic bomb.

To help meet the Soviet atomic challenge, the government began expanding Hanford, once again creating a need for more housing. David Lauder, GE's

Hanford manager, announced in August 1947 that Richland was to be enlarged to accommodate 25,000 people. He said a temporary construction town would be built five miles north of Richland to house 10,000 to 16,000 persons, including families. Barracks were moved from the old Hanford camp and from the naval station across the Columbia River to aid in housing North Richland residents. In 1948, work started on a new uptown business district in Richland; GE officials contacted many businessmen and investors to encourage their participation.

From 1947 to 1949, the federal government invested $180 million at Hanford, a little less than half the wartime expense of $350 million.

The impact of war and postwar growth was shown in 1950 census figures for incorporated towns: Richland, 21,809; Pasco, 10,228; and Kennewick, 10,106. The one-time biggest community, Hanford, still contained a few vacant buildings, but the government was selling them for removal in 1950.

Once again, an international situation jolted the Tri-Cities as U.S. forces suffered setbacks in early stages of the Korean War—a conflict destined to drag on until 1953. A new Hanford construction program was started in 1950 that boosted U.S. investment there to around $500 million. Total expenditures increased to $1 billion by 1956 after newer facilities were completed and operating.

The government added five new reactors, two chemical processing plants (Redox and Purex), and many waste storage tanks from 1947 to 1955. Anti-aircraft troops began protecting the enlarged plant. The Pasco Engineer Depot,

▲ ▲ ▲

BELOW: In 1947, construction of a trailer camp in North Richland became a top priority in an effort to house the expanded work force. On this windless day, sheets and towels dry on clotheslines across from the community shower and laundry buildings of the completed camp. These structures were built at regular intervals throughout the facility. In 1950, about 300 blacks were among the residents who lived in the barracks and trailers in North Richland. Courtesy, Atomic Energy Commission

A crowd on Lewis Street in Pasco stopped to admire the aerodynamic 1948 Tucker automobile during its promotional tour of Washington state. Despite its sleek, stylish, and powerful lines, the Tucker was unable to capture part of the market, and only 50 cars were built before the company collapsed. Courtesy, Ralph Smith

formerly known as the H&R Point, was reactivated in the Korean War and shipped equipment to ports and military bases.

Meantime, two other major developments aided Tri-Cities growth in the early 1950s—the Columbia Basin Irrigation Project and McNary Dam.

Water flowed into the Columbia Basin Project's irrigation canals in 1952 from Lake Roosevelt, the reservoir behind Grand Coulee Dam. As a result, numerous farms developed in the early 1950s as far south as Franklin County, bringing new life to small farming communities such as Mesa, Eltopia, and Connell. Some basin project farms already had been developed starting in 1948 at Pasco Heights, situated northwest of Pasco. Pasco Heights was irrigated by a temporary pumping plant, and in 1950 water was pumped to a small project area at Burbank, south of Snake River.

The other major project was the Corps of Engineers' McNary Dam, which was to be built on the Columbia River near Umatilla, Oregon, south of the Tri-Cities. Levee construction and railroad relocation in the area of the dam's planned reservoir started as early as 1949; some of this activity was near the Tri-Cities. In the small town of Wallula, all buildings had to be moved or be destroyed because they were in the area that would be inundated by the McNary reservoir. A public drawing was scheduled in 1952 so residents could draw for lots at a new town of Wallula. The major economic impact of the McNary Dam on the Tri-Cities area, outside of expanding the irrigation potential, was to help ensure barges could navigate up and down the Columbia.

The Dalles and John Day dams were completed on the Columbia River after McNary, and all of these plus Bonneville Dam provided navigation locks and reservoirs, part of a long-awaited inland waterway between Portland, Oregon, and the Tri-Cities.

Other developments that affected the Tri-Cities area included the completion of North Pacific Grain Growers Association elevators at Kennewick in 1952, the building of tanks for fuel and fertilizer for agriculture at Pasco in the early 1950s, and the building of the first of an eventual series of plants, mostly agro-chemical. The plants were located south of Kennewick and were completed in the 1950s. Walla Walla County voters approved organization of the Port of Walla Walla in 1952 to take advantage of opportunities opened by McNary reservoir; the ports of Pasco and Kennewick already had been established in 1940 and 1917 respectively.

The Lake Wallula reservoir, as the pool behind McNary was called, reached its maximum elevation in December 1953, the same month the first power from McNary was fed into the northwest power pool grid. The McNary Dam was dedicated on September 23, 1954, when President Dwight Eisenhower spoke to a crowd estimated at 35,000 to 40,000.

In addition to the basin project and dam developments, a $6.5-million four-lane-highway bridge was opened in July 1954. It spanned the Columbia River between Kennewick and Pasco. In April 1955, a bridge was completed at Umatilla, Oregon, replacing a ferry and offering easier access between Oregon and the Tri-Cities.

▲ ▲ ▲
Electricity and irrigation water were simultaneously introduced to Columbia Basin Project settlers, who lived in tents and trailers while they established farms in the area. Mrs. Ray Willingham and her family tended to household chores on a hot summer day in 1949 in the lean-to addition of their trailer on Unit 58 of the Pasco Units. Courtesy, U.S. Bureau of Reclamation

Other projects also kept construction payrolls high. In January 1956, the Corps of Engineers started work on Ice Harbor Dam, about 10 miles above the mouth of Snake River, and Grant County Public Power District began building Priest Rapids Dam in 1956 on the Columbia, about 50 miles above Richland. The Northern Pacific Railroad completed a $5.5 million new yard, containing 77 miles of track, in Pasco in 1955. And in 1958, Boise Cascade Container and Boise Cascade Kraft opened a mill at Wallula to make paper products.

Enough new housing had been built in the Tri-Cities so that North Richland was no longer required to house Hanford construction workers. So the Atomic Energy Commission (AEC) turned over North Richland to the U.S. Army in 1955. Antiaircraft troops had been guarding the atomic plant since 1950, after replacing the National Guard. Camp Hanford was established in 1950 with headquarters at North Richland. The troops manned antiaircraft guns at first and, later, missiles. After taking over all of North Richland, army families lived in housing and trailer areas formerly occupied by the construction people. The community's existence was terminated about the end of 1960 when the army camp was deactivated. Protection of the Hanford facility from air attack now became the job of the U.S. Air Force.

But the big story in the Richland area in the late 1950s was the transition of government facilities to private ownership and control. President Eisenhower

▲ ▲ ▲

At the McNary Dam site, pictured here on April 17, 1951, construction workers and engineers erected a massive powerhouse in front of the coffer dams that held back the Columbia River. The heavy concrete and metal sections of the dam were put in place by railroad cars and cranes. The entire McNary project, including levees on Lake Wallula, cost $294 million by the time of its completion. Courtesy, U.S. Army Corps of Engineers, Walla Walla District

signed a bill in 1955 for the disposal of the government-owned communities of Richland and Oak Ridge, Tennessee.

Kadlec Hospital, the community health-care facility, was transferred to the Methodist Church in 1955, and the U.S. Housing and Home Finance Agency began selling vacant Richland residential lots in early 1957. Mr. and Mrs. Paul Huckleberry bought the first house on June 20, 1957, and sales to other occupants moved ahead briskly. Also in 1957, the federal government sold the Richland telephone system to the General Telephone Company of the Northwest (now GTE Northwest, Incorporated) for about $2 million. In July 1958, residents voted for incorporation of Richland by a 4 to 1 margin, reversing an earlier vote against such a plan. School facilities were transferred from government ownership to the community in December 1958. On December 13, 1958, a simulated atomic bomb was exploded in a lot north of the uptown business district in Richland at the start of "commencement exercises," a sort of graduation ceremony at which the AEC and GE informally turned over the community to its citizens.

Richland had gone from an unincorporated, government-controlled area to a city of the first class all in the same month, reportedly the first time in Washington state history when an unincorporated area had gone immediately to first-class municipal status. Members of the first city council of the newly incorporated Richland were Paul Beardsley, Fred Brackenbush, Joyce Kelly, Lester Coon, Fred Clagett, Pat Merrill, and Ernest Street, replacing an advisory council that had actively made recommendations to the community management.

The AEC subsequently provided money to be used mostly for schools, but

also for the city and hospital. Earlier, Congress had authorized funds that were to ensure the transition from government to private control went smoothly in the Richland and Oak Ridge communities.

The possibilities of peacetime use for nuclear energy were discussed extensively in the late 1950s, and Hanford's first big project in this field was a plutonium recycle test reactor, authorized by the U.S. Congress in 1958. The reactor was constructed between 1958 and 1961. In 1959, work also started on a new plutonium plant, the N-reactor, costing $195,200,000.

Washington senators Henry Jackson and Warren Magnuson were among regional leaders getting federal funds for Hanford projects, working closely with the Tri-City Nuclear Industrial Council.

Richland's transition continued with the turnover of the library, recreation department, water and sewage system, other public works, and the electrical distribution system in 1959. A city hall was dedicated on December 12, 1959, and Murrey Fuller took over duties as city manager in the same year, the second city manager in the Tri-Cities. In 1955 Bill Hansen had also begun acting as city manager in Kennewick. Of the three cities, Pasco was the last to hire a city manager, in 1964, when Horace Menasco started duties.

The sale of a Richland house in May 1960 to Everett McGhan was the last in the Richland and Oak Ridge changeover. A total of 3,788 single-family residences and 1,018 two-family houses had been sold at Richland for about $30 million. Some commercial properties and undeveloped land were still on sale. In 1960, Richland still led the Tri-Cities in population with 23,548 residents. Kennewick contained 14,244 people and Pasco 14,522, while 1,347 residents lived in West Richland, incorporated in 1955.

Look magazine named Richland an "All-American city" in 1961 for its transition efforts. "Though many householders preferred the easy paternalism of government operation, a 10-year citizen-led campaign finally convinced the

▲ ▲ ▲

The McNary powerhouse interior contains turbine generators. As the water flows under the dam, many feet below the river's surface, it rotates the turbine, which spins the shaft and rotor, producing the electricity. Here, the rotor for the sixth unit is shown being assembled. A total of 14 generators were installed by 1957. Courtesy, U.S. Army Corps of Engineers, Walla Walla District

▲ ▲ ▲

Local native Harry Jim objected to the building of Ice Harbor Dam in 1959, asking that the scattering of his people's bones be halted. His father, Fishhook Jim, had tried to protect the burial sites of some 3,000 Walla Walla Indians on the Rocky and Main islands in the Snake River by filing a homestead claim for 116 acres near Fishhook Bend. Courtesy, Ted Van Arsdol

majority that independence was best," the magazine noted.

On May 9, 1962, Vice-President Lyndon Johnson stopped off for the dedication of Ice Harbor Dam and stressed the need to conserve the nation's resources. With this project completed, Tri-Cities residents were optimistic that development of other dams on the lower Snake River would move ahead. Lower Monumental Dam, the next project upstream, was completed in 1969, and two other dams below Lewiston, Idaho, were also built.

One of 1962's big events for the Tri-Cities area was President John Kennedy's signing of a bill approving a dual-purpose (plutonium production and power) reactor at Hanford. This project had been debated for several years after General Electric Co. had proposed the plant. Opponents did not want an electric power facility connected to the N-reactor. However, Congress had compromised with the Eisenhower administration when the original authorization for the reactor had been approved. The compromise set aside $25 million out of the total amount ($145 million) that had been designated for the original construction of the reactor. The $25 million would permit later conversion of the reactor to power production, in addition to its role producing plutonium.

But the fight had continued. Power conversion opponents were "private utility and coal lobbyists and 'save-the-industries' shouters of other regions," the *Portland Oregonian* reported in 1961. For months the bill "was pushed around in Congress like the frail heroine in the clutches of movie landlords and other vipers," the *Washington Teamster* remarked.

One of the main promoters for the dual-purpose reactor had been the Tri-City Nuclear Industrial Council, formed in February 1963, with R.F. Philip as president. The group's goal was to diversify Hanford's defense mission and gain more industry and payrolls for the Tri-Cities by less dependency on the federal payroll.

Less than two months before his assassination, President Kennedy arrived for the ground-breaking ceremony for the N-reactor's power-generating facility. Kennedy told a crowd of 40,000 on September 26, 1963, that the nation was "forging not a sword but a plowshare" in the Hanford conversion. The President waved an atomic pointer at a radiation-counting device, which activated an automatic 60-foot crane that started the digging.

The federal government was paying for the N-reactor, and a state agency

called the Washington Public Power Supply System (WPPSS) was financing the power-generating facility. WPPSS was an agency established by the Washington state legislature, specifically so that public utility districts could pool their resources and efforts when constructing power projects.

The first power at the generating plant was produced in April 1966.

In 1965, the Atomic Energy Commission moved into a new seven-story federal building in Richland, replacing temporary wooden structures. This building housed the post office, a federal courtroom, and offices, in addition to the AEC and its contractors. Sam Volpentest, president of the Richland Chamber of Commerce in 1960, proposed the building, called Project X at that time.

Another 1965 improvement was the opening of the 22-mile, two-lane Hanford highway from Horn Rapids on the Yakima River to Vernita on the Columbia River, located on the north side of the Hanford area. In addition, a bridge was opened at Vernita. In 1967, a 6.5-mile link from Stevens Drive in Richland to Horn Rapids was completed.

The late 1960s brought considerable transition to the Hanford project. A major reason was a government cutback in plutonium production, both at Savannah River, South Carolina, and Hanford. Glenn Seaborg, AEC chairman at the time, said President Johnson called him in shortly after Kennedy's death and told him to "start cutting back." The budget had to be balanced, Johnson explained. From December 1964 to 1970, seven of the eight older reactors at Hanford were shut down.

New contractors also moved in during 1965, when General Electric Company's contract expired. The AEC thought segmentation of the Hanford activity would encourage diversification; the new contractors were required to support projects that would bring new industries and businesses to the Tri-Cities.

Residents were heartened in 1967 by news that the AEC had picked Hanford as the site of a Fast Flux Test Facility (FFTF), the AEC's major fuels and materials test irradiation facility in the Liquid Metal Fast Breeder Reactor (LMFBR) program. This would contribute as well to other programs: The AEC wanted to demonstrate the capability of commercial large-size breeder power

▲ ▲ ▲

Richland's transfer from government ownership to local control was celebrated in a three-day festival. The commencement exercises began on December 13, 1958, when a simulated atomic bomb, prepared by U.S. Army personnel at Camp Hanford and detonated by E.J. Bloch of the Atomic Energy Commission, exploded in uptown Richland. Courtesy, Ralph Smith

▲ ▲ ▲

One of the challenges of working with nuclear fuel and waste is the creation of remote-control operations to manipulate and monitor the processes that are too radioactive for human exposure. Workers in protective clothing are shown in the late 1950s, inserting a plastic-covered camera into a waste storage tank where it will be rotated to take pictures of the interior conditions. Courtesy, General Electric

plants. Construction started on the FFTF in 1970.

The late 1960s also was an era of Vietnam War protests and restlessness among minorities in the cities. Many blacks had taken construction jobs in the Hanford boom days, and a considerable number remained. Most of these residents lived in east Pasco. Much publicity was focused on racial tensions as the result of a minor riot at Kurtzman Park at Pasco in 1967; during the riot, four Pasco policemen were injured. The brawl followed a lengthy verbal conflict between police and east Pasco residents. A federal investigation, agreed to by the Pasco City Council, was launched, and a community relations office was opened in east Pasco.

An urban renewal project, approved in 1968 and completed in the early 1970s, was backed by the U.S. Department of Housing and Urban Development and with limited city funds. The effort involved commercial and industrial development in the east Pasco area that had been cleared of substandard homes. The *Tri-City Herald* called the project, Pasco's "most obvious and dramatic positive achievement in the 1960s."

In west Kennewick, the Columbia Center shopping mall opened near the area called the Richland Y in October 1969. The center advertised "55 stores all under one roof" and hoped to draw customers from the Columbia Basin Project, Yakima Valley, Dayton, Walla Walla, and the Hermiston-Pendleton area in Oregon. This hope was realized.

Food processing plants were increasing in the area to take care of output from newly irrigated farms. In 1970, nearly 1,600 persons worked in such plants, up 35 percent from 1969 and up 60 percent from 1968. Populations in 1970 numbered 15,212 in Kennewick, 13,920 in Pasco, and 26,290 in Richland.

In 1970, Sam Volpentest, Tri-City Nuclear Industrial Council vice-president, told about efforts "to sell utilities and state and local officials on the desirability and practicability of establishing a nuclear power park at Hanford."

But the next year started in a gloomy way at Hanford. President Richard Nixon announced in January that he was cutting funds for all defense materials

▲ ▲ ▲

Richland's first city council stood attentively behind Governor Albert Rosellini while he addressed the crowd that gathered at the Columbia High School on December 13, 1958. From left to right are, Mayor Pat Merrill, Fred Brackenbush, Ernie Street, Joyce Kelly, Lester Coon, Paul Beardsley, and Fred Clagett. Courtesy, Ralph Smith

production at Hanford. Apparently he believed reactors in South Carolina could do the job of supplying sufficient plutonium for the nation's needs. The cutback affected the last old reactor, K-East, and the N-reactor with its power-generating facility. Hanford supporters rallied, and in April the Nixon administration agreed to continue dual-purpose operations. But the WPPSS had to reimburse the government for the steam, which was a by-product from the N-reactor. In September, President Nixon visited Hanford and talked to a large crowd about the nation's fast breeder reactor program.

Closure of the oldest reactors also resulted in the moth-balling in 1972 of the Purex plant, a chemical processing facility. Federally-funded Hanford operating employment dipped from 8,300 in 1969 to between 5,000 and 6,000.

Prior to the 1970s, the accumulating nuclear wastes stored at Hanford had not been a subject of much public note, although leaks had developed for several years. The biggest leak consisted of 115,000 gallons of nuclear wastes from the processing of plutonium, which had sunk into the soil beneath one of the storage tanks. This leak focused attention on the waste management issue in 1973. A major effort was started to upgrade waste storage.

In the research field, energy had become a major focus at Hanford by the mid-1970s. Hanford personnel studied possible future uses of nuclear, solar, geothermal, fossil, wind, and organic waste energy.

The continuing interest of private companies in Hanford efforts was reflected by Exxon Nuclear's purchase of the Donald W. Douglas Laboratories, which became the Exxon Research and Technology Center.

But the biggest story developing for the Tri-Cities in the 1970s was another construction boom. During the 1970s, the Tri-Cities were destined to be one of the fastest-growing communities in the nation. Labor analyst Dean

Ice Harbor Dam construction began in January 1956 and included major changes to the surrounding area. The river channel had to be excavated for six miles downstream to allow for barge passage and 57 miles of railroad track above the dam had to be relocated to higher ground. The initial cost of the 2,790-foot dam was $130 million. Courtesy, U.S. Army Corps of Engineers, Walla Walla District

Schau said the total number of jobs in the area grew by more than 90 percent from 1972 to 1979.

A major factor was the WPPSS decision to build three reactors at Hanford. Work on the first reactor (plant 2) started in 1972, and by the mid-1970s, a go-ahead was given to build two more reactors. The total cost of the project was estimated at $3 billion, and the first plant was expected to be operating by 1978 or 1979. In 1975, Columbia Foods, Inc., reopened the former Cudahy plant, a meat processing facility that had closed about 1973. This was adjacent to John McGregor's big livestock feed lot at Wallula.

All through the Tri-Cities, construction was booming, with Kennewick leading the way. "The area along Clearwater Avenue, Highway 14, and Vista Way, known just as Clearwater, is the busiest, fastest-growing new area in town, and probably in the Tri-Cities," a 1976 news story commented. Work was under way on the Highlands Shopping Center, once the site of orchards, farms, and vineyards. New apartment complexes were popular, and homes were beginning to climb the Horse Heaven Hills, where the city of Kennewick was having trouble extending water lines and maintaining sufficient pressure to provide water at higher elevations.

The U.S. census of retail establishments in 1977 reflected this growth in Kennewick—375 retail firms, with sales of $213,161,000. Richland had 221 retail sales firms with $91,964,000, and Pasco had 219 retail firms; sales value at Pasco was not listed.

Fast Flux Test Facility construction was completed by the end of 1978, and fuel was loaded for the first time in 1979. However, the facility achieved initial nuclear start-up in 1980, and with a series of start-up tests and equipment check-outs, the operating cycle started in 1982. FFTF was called the world's most advanced and versatile test reactor. Late in 1978, work started on another important Hanford project, the Fuels and Materials Examination Facility (FMEF). FMEF's objective was to provide fuel to the FFTF.

By 1978-79, Hanford's work force had soared to more than 20,000. About half of the work force was in construction, including the WPPSS employees. This was more than three times the 1971-72 Hanford employee total. WPPSS cost estimates had increased greatly, and the first reactor now was not scheduled for completion until 1981. In addition to three Hanford reactors, the WPPSS was constructing two reactors at Satsop in Grays Harbor County, Washington. Neil Strand, WPPSS managing director, admitted that WPPSS had not be-lieved the job would get so large and com-plex so quickly.

In March 1979, a severe reactor accident at Three-Mile Island in Pennsylvania drew nationwide publicity, and began to cast a shadow over the nuclear industry. News-paper stories in the summer publicized the fact that truckloads of Three-Mile nuclear wastes were to be hauled to Hanford, thus focusing more attention on the waste stor-age issue in the central Washington desert.

Non-nuclear projects continued to help the area for a while. Boise Cascade Corpo-ration completed a plant expansion at Wal-lula in 1980, totaling $275 million. Also in 1980, Iowa Beef Processors finished $20 million in improvements; this was at the Wallula plant formerly called Columbia Foods.

The 1980 census confirmed the big impact of the 1970s on area growth. Kennewick now led with 34,397 residents, more than double its population of 10 years earlier; Richland was second with 33,578; and Pasco trailed with 18,425. West Richland had 2,938 residents.

In 1980, a lengthy strike proved costly to WPPSS. News stories reported huge cost overruns and construction delays for the five WPPSS reactors, called the biggest construction and financial venture in Washington state his-tory. Bob Ferguson, who had directed advanced reactor technology for the Department of Energy, was called in during August to try and turn the tide. The *New York Times* reported Ferguson and a cadre of seasoned aides "have moved with the precision of a SWAT squad" to rescue WPPSS. But they faced many problems including financial; meantime media critics and part of the Pacific Northwest's citizenry were expressing concern over the safety of nu-clear power and waste disposal.

This peak period of construction crisis coincided, unfortunately, with a na-tional recession. Unemployment was rising, while inflation, which stood at

▲ ▲ ▲
The U.S. Army protected the defense operations of Hanford with anti-aircraft missiles in the late 1950s. Less labor intensive than anti-aircraft guns, the missiles could be fired from a protected area. German shepherds were trained to respond to hand commands and assisted in patrolling the grounds. Courtesy, Ted Van Arsdol

more than 12 percent in 1980, rose to 14 percent in 1981. In addition, area farmers had been affected severely by national economic conditions.

Total Hanford employment reached 25,000 in 1981 and 26,000 in May 1982; a little more than half of this increase was from WPPSS work. "Traffic nightmare," blared a newspaper headline describing rush-hour congestion between Hanford, the three cities, and their outlying areas. Contractors staggered employee hours in 1981, and this helped traffic somewhat.

Construction was stopped in late 1981 on WPPSS' fourth reactor plant at Hanford, and in April 1982 the power system accepted a Bonneville Power Administration decision to stop work on Plant 1. Construction also ceased at the two Satsop plants, and payrolls plummeted. In 1983, WPPSS defaulted on its bonds for two of the plants.

Many of the thousands of construction workers laid off by WPPSS left the area. Unemployment was high for many months, and real estate sales dropped dramatically.

WPPSS did manage to complete the Hanford Plant 2 reactor, which opened in December 1984. The FMEF also was completed in late 1984.

Early in 1985 the name of the Tri-City Nuclear Industrial Council was changed to Tri-City Industrial Development Council (TRIDEC). Ferguson, a TRIDEC official explained: "TCNIC was identified in the minds of many solely with the Hanford nuclear programs." Also in 1985, TRIDEC merged with the Tri-Cities Chamber of Commerce, to become the major organization aimed at economic development and diversification of the area.

Under the Reagan administration, Hanford's role shifted to again stress defense production. Sixty percent of funding for Hanford was for national defense and the rest for research and related programs. In 1986, the Department

▲ ▲ ▲

Columbia Center stood alone in the middle of the desert when developers with vision established a regional shopping mall midway between Kennewick and Richland in 1969. The runway in the background was part of the Kennewick Airport at Vista Field. Columbia Center Boulevard, barely visible in the middle of this picture, is now a busy four-lane thoroughfare lined with stores—one of the busiest growth areas in the Tri-Cities region. Courtesy, **Tri-City Herald**

Exuberant Tri-Cities developers participated in the groundbreaking ceremony for a $3.5 million shopping center on Highway 395 in Kennewick on November 23, 1975. Construction of the Highland Shopping Center was completed a year later when Albertsons became the first store to open on December 15, 1976. **Courtesy, Tri-City Herald**

of Energy (in charge at Hanford since 1975) released 40 years of Hanford environmental data to the public. The Chernobyl nuclear accident in the Soviet Union occurred in April, and this brought what a department official called "a deluge of international media requests for information." Critics compared Hanford's N-reactor with the Chernobyl facility, but Hanford officials pointed out important differences between the two reactors.

In December 1986, the Department of Energy announced a "standdown" of the N-reactor for six months of safety enhancements. But this did not satisfy some of the public. Considerable opposition to the reactor had developed among environmentalists, anti-nuclear groups, and some politicians; in February 1988 the department reported that the reactor was being placed in "cold standby." Support facilities also were affected by the continuing closure.

Hanford was in the news, too, as the result of a controversy over selection of a national, high-level nuclear waste repository. Final choices were narrowed down to Hanford, a Texas site, and the Yucca Mountain vicinity in Nevada. In late 1987, Congress voted to eliminate Hanford and Texas sites from consideration and ordered the Department of Energy to focus attention on Nevada.

The combined effect of the WPPSS decline and N-reactor shutdown brought much foreboding, in addition to immediate job losses. However, the communities joined in a cooperative spirit to meet the new challenges, and the *Tri-City Herald* reported late in 1989 that "all economic indicators point to a revitalized economy." Retail sales were strong, 1,600 more persons were working at Hanford than had been projected in 1988, mostly because of an increased waste management program, and agriculture was providing a stabilizing element.

CHAPTER FIVE

Old and New Enterprises

▲ ▲ ▲

An early slogan, "Keep Your Eye on Pasco," had survived from the early 1900s and was on view when the writer of this book passed through town for the first time, shortly before World War II. Some visitors must have thought this worth a chuckle or snicker considering that Pasco was a small place in a vast expanse of brown, often dusty landscape. But the long-ago slogan makers have proved to be visionaries, assessing well the Tri-Cities' potential.

In four decades the massive Columbia Basin Irrigation Project has been more than one-half completed north of the Tri-Cities and now totals 550,000 acres. The Kennewick division of the federal Yakima Irrigation Project has been developed, and more than 200,000 acres in Benton, Franklin, and Walla

Walla counties are receiving irrigation water from private projects, while big private ventures also have blossomed on the Oregon side of the Columbia River, near McNary Dam.

And the economy continues to benefit from Hanford. Although the last production reactor was closed in 1988, Hanford remains a vital research center with nuclear materials processing plants, waste management responsibilities, and continuing energy research.

New bridges over the Columbia River and completion of an interstate highway in the 1980s, linking the Tri-Cities with the Ellensburg area and with an interstate route in Oregon, are major transportation developments. Slack-water navigation on the Columbia and Snake rivers keeps barge business good, and

▲ ▲ ▲

Irrigation water reached this field in Unit 19 of Block 17 in Franklin County in the summer of 1964, enabling Darryl Hulse and his son Blaine to choose from a variety of irrigated crops. The sprinkling system pictured here rolls through the field, assuring even water distribution for the alfalfa they would plant the following weekend. Photo by Ron York/U.S. Bureau of Reclamation

▲ ▲ ▲

The flood of 1948 brought the Columbia River halfway up the wheels of this truck on Avenue C, which is now known as Columbia Drive in Kennewick. Volunteers removed merchandise from flooded stores and National Guardsmen patrolled the flooded areas. More than 1,000 families were forced from their homes. Courtesy, Ralph Smith

the Tri-Cities also has one of the state's major airports at Pasco.

Sprawling growth and easier transportation have brought the communities closer together. Politically, they have gone their separate ways, and consolidation proposals have been voted down. But instances of cooperation in a variety of civic efforts are common.

In land size, the Columbia Basin Irrigation Project remains dominant in the region. The South Columbia Basin Irrigation District, with headquarters at Pasco, takes in more than one-third of the project—about 226,000 irrigated acres in 1989. This is mostly in Franklin County, with some acreage in Adams and Grant counties and a little in Walla Walla County.

Basin farmers have tried a variety of crops. Sugar beet production plummeted after closure of Utah-Idaho Sugar Company (U&I) processing plants at Toppenish and Moses Lake in 1979, but other crops have taken their place. Potato crops rank high in output—Franklin County was second in the state in potato production in 1988, just behind Grant County (also in the Basin Project) and Benton County took third place. Corn and wheat output are up, and plantings of asparagus, grapes, apples, and other fruit increased greatly in the 1980s.

Most south district fruit is grown on the Wahluke Slope north of Hanford. The slope, with southern exposure and more frost-free days than most other areas, has been called "the fruit basket of the Columbia Basin."

One facility that could aid further reclamation in Franklin County is extension of the East Low Canal. This canal would carry water southward from Banks Lake to land in the northern part of the county. Enlargement of the canal, in a northern part of the project, is scheduled to start in the 1990s, and construction of the extension would follow a number of years later, if the long-range plan is followed.

The U.S. Bureau of Reclamation, in charge of the basin project, was talking in the late 1980s about investigating possible nonfederal development. Up to now, the project has been entirely a federal undertaking.

In addition to the federal basin project progress in Franklin County, private irrigation has been providing water since early 1989 for 60,000 to 70,000 acres, mostly in the eastern part of the county. Bill Ford, agronomy extension agent at Pasco, said the irrigation water comes from the Snake River and wells. Crop trends are the same as in the federal project—a lot of diversified agriculture and a significant increase in fruit.

An area north of Pasco and just south of the basin project has been called "the Green Belt" because of the advent of private irrigation from wells 100 to 300 feet deep on both sides of Highway 395. But the water table has been falling in the Smith Canyon area, east of the highway.

Much of the private irrigation development near the Tri-Cities stems from completion of the giant reservoirs behind Ice Harbor and McNary dams. The pools are close to arable land and relatively stable, so pumping stations are feasible.

Construction of these facilities started in the 1960s. "It seemed like all we did was fight sand," said Keith Ellis, a developer trying to bring water to Eureka Flat in Walla Walla County from Ice Harbor reservoir in the late 1960s. U&I was among the leaders in private irrigation, with its biggest push in the

▲ ▲ ▲

Wheat continued to be a major dryland crop in the Horse Heaven Hills to the south of Kennewick. Contour plowing on the slopes, as pictured here in the late 1950s, protected the topsoil from erosion and created interesting designs in the fields. Planted in the fall, winter wheat took advantage of all available soil moisture and was harvested in midsummer. Photo by Howard Woodworth. Courtesy, Ted Van Arsdol

Horse Heaven Hills of Benton County. By the early 1980s, the private development boom had ended. Reporter Bob Woehler summed up the situation: "The costs of water, electricity to pump the water and land all have risen at a greater rate than the price a farmer gets for his crops." Also, much of the land that was easiest to reach and cheaper to develop was already irrigated.

Some Benton County land is served from the Columbia River, and other property gets water from wells or the Yakima River. More than 96,000 acres were in private projects by the end of 1988, and 68,000 county acres were part of the Yakima project in either the Roza, Sunnyside, or the Kennewick divisions. Jack Watson, Benton County extension agent, reported "a pretty dramatic shift" in the last 15 to 20 years. Farmers have gone from growing crops such as sugar beets, potatoes, small grain, and hay to growing fairly high income crops on irrigated lands, such as hops, mint, asparagus, apples, cherries, and carrots.

Watson does not see an increase in Benton County land irrigated from the Yakima River: "We're taxed now to get water to the various entities. We might see enhancement of the existing development through more efficient use." A large number of wells were drilled in the county in 1988 because of drought concerns, mostly in the Roza area, which has a junior water right. Older irrigation projects have first rights to the river water.

The biggest irrigation project getting electricity from Benton County PUD is an AgriNorthwest farm in the Horse Heaven Hills. The PUD provides electricity to 70,000 acres in private projects, which is used for pumping plants and driving pivot irrigation.

One of the county's oldest projects is the Columbia Irrigation District, successor to the pioneering Kennewick enterprise of the 1890s. The canal from

Yakima River now reaches seven miles south of Kennewick to the Hover area; it had extended further south, but part was cut off by changes resulting from the filling of the pool behind McNary Dam.

Among the results from irrigation has been the development of a wine industry. Washington state is second to California in production of viniferous grapes, and the state's main concentration of wineries is in south central Washington. About 15 wineries are situated in the Tri-Cities, Benton City, and Prosser vicinities, and most offer tours and wine-tasting. More wineries can be found further up Yakima Valley. The area's top wines are said to rival Europe's best.

Dryland-farming agriculture also is not overlooked. Farmers using fertilizers and other modern horticultural methods have made the Tri-Cities an important dryland-farming area, ironically on land where many early homesteaders failed. Around 226,000 acres were planted with wheat in Benton and Franklin counties in 1988, mostly in the dry areas.

A variety of food processing plants have been established in the Tri-Cities area. Ports in the area have been interested in the success of such businesses and have issued industrial revenue bonds to help several of these plants.

Even irrigation to grow a forest has been considered among the economic possibilities of the area. In 1970, agricultural economist Bruce Cone concluded that an irrigated cottonwood or sycamore forest at Hanford could be economically feasible, although risky. The proposal would involve harvesting trees every five years and using the chips in an adjacent pulp mill. Apparently no updated cost studies have been made in recent years.

One of the biggest tree-planting projects on the arid lands was GE's "shelter belt" of the 1950s, grown on the west side of Richland to protect residents from sandstorms. In January 1990, half these trees were blown down in a windstorm.

The Hanford nuclear plant continues a major economic underpinning of the Tri-Cities area. The security, relative isolation, and large area that can be used for development are factors helpful for some possible projects. The experienced work force and facilities already developed are other assets of the 560-square-mile government site. Thirteen thousand persons were working at Hanford in early 1990—nearly 9,000 of these were employees of one firm, Westinghouse Hanford Company.

In 1989 Hanford was one of three sites in the United States to be considered in 1992 for a new light-water reactor, producing

▲ ▲ ▲

ABOVE: The agricultural roots of the mid-Columbia region and the "can-do" attitude of its residents are evident in this youngster's face as she tries to get her pig to pose for the camera at the Benton-Franklin County Fair. Every summer the area pauses to participate in the week-long festivities and to enjoy agricultural and livestock displays and big-name entertainment. Courtesy, **Tri-City Herald**

▲ ▲ ▲

Here, two teams of Hanford reactor operators prepare to charge the 100K West Reactor in the late 1950s. The movable work platform permitted access to all parts of the reactor face including 3,000 process tubes. As a fresh fuel element was inserted into a process tube, the irradiated element was discharged at the rear face of the reactor. Courtesy, General Electric

tritium for the U.S. nuclear weapons program.

Some Hanford proponents have suggested that the Washington Public Power Supply System's Plant 1 reactor, two-thirds completed when construction stopped, could be converted to the tritium producer. Another possibility would be the building of a heavy-water reactor or high-temperature gas-cooled reactor at the Skagit/Hanford site, five miles west of the WPPSS reactor complex. Puget Sound Power and Light Co. wanted to construct a plant at the site, and some preliminary planning was completed.

Hanford's N-reactor, which produced plutonium and electricity, was closed indefinitely in 1988 after much publicity and controversy that occurred in the aftermath of the Chernobyl nuclear disaster in the Soviet Union. Environmentalists and anti-nuclear groups cited comparisons between the Hanford and Chernobyl reactors.

Michael J. Lawrence, Department of Energy manager at Hanford, said both the reactors have the same superficial attributes as an airplane or a car. "They both have engines, wheels and seats." But Lawrence said many different design and operating procedures exist that would preclude a Chernobyl-type accident from occurring at the reactor. However, "the damage was done" by the criticism, according to Lawrence, and department officials announced the reactor's temporary closure for safety upgrading. The reactor was closed permanently in 1988 because plutonium was no longer needed.

In July 1988, the department reported Hanford's Fast Flux Test Facility would be used to produce plutonium 238 isotopes to provide power for space capsules in interplanetary travel and for underwater surveillance by the navy.

Plans were under way to demonstrate metal fuel for advanced reactors and components for space power systems. Future applications in fusion, isotope production, by-product heat utilization, waste management, and plutonium destruction in support of arms reduction were mentioned.

But in January 1990, the Department of Energy proposed closing the FFTF over a five-year period and said that agency would produce plutonium 238 at Savannah River, South Carolina. FFTF backers started an effort to save the Hanford reactor.

Cleanup of nuclear wastes at Hanford has been one phase of a nationwide discussion involving the various Department of Energy nuclear sites. U.S.

energy secretary, James D. Watkins, has said Hanford will be "the flagship" of the Department of Energy waste cleanup and technology. Extensive government appropriations will be required for this effort. One plant scheduled for Hanford, costing nearly $1 billion, will turn liquid and solid nuclear wastes into glass. This waste vitrification plant will be completed by 1998.

Tentative proposals for the future of Hanford's unused, contaminated reactors and chemical processing facilities are to take them apart and bury them, or entomb the huge structures under tons of earth and concrete; either way will require an extensive effort.

The Association of Washington Business has taken note of Hanford's important national and state role. In 1988, the group called for conversion of WPPSS' Plant 1 for tritium production, establishment of a $135-million Molecular Science Center at Hanford as proposed by Battelle Northwest, assignment of a long-term mission to the FFTF, and accelerated cleanup of nuclear and hazardous wastes at Hanford.

Meanwhile along the Columbia River, plans are continuing for hydroelectric projects that could affect the Tri-Cities area. For example the Walla Walla district of the U.S. Army's Corps of Engineers plans to build a second powerhouse at McNary Dam, with a capacity of 742,000 kilowatts. These plans also include provisions that will compensate for fish and wildlife depletion and improve the levee at Pasco, Kennewick, and Richland. The pool behind McNary Dam, called Lake Wallula, extends for 64 miles; slack water reaches to the Columbia at Richland and to the Snake at Ice Harbor Dam.

▲ ▲ ▲

Tanks like these under construction in 1944 were built to house byproducts of the original plutonium production process. They were surrounded by reinforced concrete and buried underground. Handling this legacy of nuclear waste, with its continuing chemical changes, is one of the current challenges of the nuclear industry. Courtesy, Hanford Science Center

▲ ▲ ▲

Clover Island was almost barren except for the Coast Guard station in this circa 1954 view, as it rose above the newly diked Lake Wallula. Half of the superstructure on the partially completed highway bridge spans the water between Kennewick and Pasco. Richland and the Hanford Engineer Works are barely visible in front of Rattlesnake Mountain. Photo by Howard Woodworth. Courtesy, Ted Van Arsdol

A new, larger navigation lock is under construction at Bonneville Dam on the lower Columbia. When completed by the Corps of Engineers in 1993, this lock will provide capacity similar to locks already in use further east on the Columbia and lower Snake rivers. This will increase commercial shipping capabilities on the Columbia.

The stretch of Columbia River above Richland, called the Hanford Reach, remains in a natural state. A proposal dating from the 1950s calls for the development of a dam above Richland on the upper Columbia. Although the proposal has won support from backers of navigation, it has faced opposition from fish, wildlife, and recreation groups.

In 1988 the U.S. Congress passed legislation calling for a Department of Interior study to determine if the Hanford Reach should be designated as a recreational area or as a wild and scenic stretch of river, needing preservation. Under the legislation, the Hanford Reach would be protected for eight years, and Congress would consider the study recommendations. Meantime the Corps of Engineers is prohibited from major dredging.

Engineers have studied a proposal to build a bypass canal, which would be used for navigation and hydropower. The canal would be constructed through Hanford, thereby leaving the river in its natural state. The corps has also investigated the possibility of building European-type ship locks so that barges could be hoisted over Priest Rapids and Wanapum dams, located above Hanford.

The ports of Kennewick, Pasco, and Walla Walla and the Walla Walla Grain Growers, Inc., are enjoying the continuing benefits of slack-water navigation. Grain is the main product hauled downstream, while petroleum products are predominately shipped upstream. Containerized cargo has been a trend for more than a decade.

On the shore of the Columbia extending south of Kennewick, a series of industrial plants was constructed starting in the 1950s. These are mostly "agrochem" (fertilizer) plants, with some manufacturing. Sue Watkins, believed to be the state's first woman port manager, took over here in 1975. The Port of Pasco operates Big Pasco Industrial Park at the former Engineer Depot, and has provided a container terminal since 1976. The port also is in charge of one of the state's major passenger and cargo airports—the Tri-Cities Airport—north of Pasco. In acreage, the airport is the third largest in the state. A new terminal building was dedicated at the airport in 1986.

The Port of Benton is the area's newest port, established in 1958 and encompassing the western three-quarters of Benton County. This port operates industrial parks at Richland, Prosser, and Benton City and airports at Prosser and Richland. More than 40 businesses were situated on port property at the start of 1989.

New highways have had a big impact on area development. One example was a surge of commercial development at Angus Village on Kennewick Highlands in response to construction of a highway interchange and overpass linking with the new cloverleaf and "blue bridge" on the Columbia River; the new section of road was opened in September 1956. Angus Village was the forerunner of other commercial development in the Highlands area.

The biggest new project with continuing significant impact is Interstate Highway 82 through central Washington with an extension (state Route 182) to Pasco. The 132.5-mile section, which extends from a tie-in with Interstate 90 at Ellensburg to Plymouth in Benton County on the Columbia River, cost nearly $380 million. An additional 14.4 miles from Goose Gap Junction to Pasco's Oregon Street cost nearly $124 million. State Route 182, built from

▲ ▲ ▲

Visitors to the Pasco Airport today see a sleek modern terminal that bears no resemblance to this 1930 photograph of the airport's early facilities. State-of-the-art equipment in the early 1930s included a nine-million-candlepower revolving beacon light, a 20,000-watt floodlight, and an illuminated windsock. The unpaved landing field was oiled to ensure a smooth and safe landing. Courtesy, Franklin County Historical Society

FACING PAGE: The Benton County
Justice Center in Prosser provides
a central focus of local county gov-
ernment and services in the Tri-
Cities area, in conjunction with the
recently built county facilities in
Kennewick. Photo by Harold
Pleasant

1981 to 1984, includes two Columbia River bridges between Pasco and
Richland, one named for newspaper publisher Glenn C. Lee and the other
for Sam Volpentest of TRIDEC.

The first stretch of I-82, opened in 1971 after 10 years of construction, was
the Ellensburg-Yakima link, which bypasses a winding Yakima Canyon road.
Modifications to the Columbia River bridge at the southern end of I-82 were
scheduled for completion in 1990.

TRIDEC and the Yakima County Development Association believe completion of I-82 has opened new potential for growth. They point out that access
by motor vehicles to this section of the state is now much easier, land is cheap
and plentiful east of the mountains, and a large labor force is available to industries. Promotion of the Tri-Cities area seems timely, especially when considering current trends, as has the Federal Reserve Bank of San Francisco. The
bank noted in late 1988 in a weekly newsletter that

Increases in the costs of labor and real estate eventually force firms to
seek areas with slack labor markets. For example, western Washing-
ton and the areas around San Francisco and Los Angeles have ex-
panded rapidly in recent years. Now these areas are imposing limits
on further growth, and employers are complaining of labor shortages.
As a result, the rate of growth is rising in parts of the West where
labor is more plentiful, such as eastern Washington, Idaho, Utah and
central California.

The Tri-Cities transportation situation continues to be aided by railroads,
which provided the first significant impetus for growth. Burlington Northern
and Union Pacific lines serve the area, and AMTRAK trains stop at Pasco.
Railroad employment in the area was more than 400 in 1990.

Among the Tri-Cities, Richland is still the home of most Hanford nuclear
plant employees; many of these are scientists and engineers. The number of
Hanford employees has been much steadier than the construction employment
payroll. For fiscal year 1989 the number of Hanford employees totaled 11,400.
Richland has modernized considerably and enlarged since the sale of homes
and other property by the federal government.

In Pasco a farmers market has drawn people to the downtown since 1985.
Some come looking for field-fresh products, others for fresh fruits and vegetables, and others for antiques, arts, and crafts. The market draws a large crowd
that reflects the Tri-Cities diverse population of Hispanics, Blacks, Caucasians,
and Asians.

This project was implemented by the Pasco Downtown Development
Association, which has been leading efforts to revitalize the older business
section. Business interest in this section suffered as people began using highways built around the downtown. Commercial development is now more dis-
persed, partly as a result of new highway construction. Because of its location

near the new highways, Court Street is a busy business area, and several auto dealers have established a sales area west of Highway 395.

Since the late 1970s, Kennewick's biggest dream was building a Tri-Cities Coliseum. Completion of this project was delayed after the economic downturn of 1981-82, but the coliseum finally was finished in late 1988 by Continental Sports Corp. The coliseum was designed as the home of the Tri-City Americans of the Western Hockey League, but soon was made available for other events too.

In 1988 the city's commercial position was enhanced by a $15-million remodeling of Columbia Center shopping mall by the Edward J. DeBartolo Corporation, one of the mall owners. In 1988 Lamonts, Inc., and Sears Roebuck and Co. moved to the mall during new construction, and the total number of new stores was increased to about 90.

Kennewick's long-frustrated effort to be a seat of county government also has been partially realized. Benton County residents had defeated a proposal in 1976 to move the county seat from Prosser to Richland, but in 1979 county voters approved construction of county courtrooms and jails at Kennewick. The $11-million structure was built in the early 1980s, providing several county offices, in addition to courtrooms and a jail. However, the courthouse in Prosser was improved during the decade as well, since the two communities share county government duties.

Consolidation of the three cities into one has been difficult. Such a plan was voted down in 1985, with only Richland providing a majority in favor. Opposition in Pasco was so strong that a vote scheduled in 1988 listed only Kennewick and Richland. The majority of residents in Kennewick were opposed; Richland residents liked the idea. No name for the merged town was advanced officially. The vote result left the Tri-Cities name as an appropriate designation—one that may be in use for at least a few more years.

CHAPTER SIX

Give Us Your Puddled Masses

▲ ▲ ▲

I n publicizing the area, Tri-Cities promoters have stressed that the sun
shines about 300 days each year. This is a definite asset when comparing
the area to the cloudier, wetter country west of the Cascade Mountains,
where most of Washington state's population resides. Advertising for the Tri-
Cities several years ago, aimed at coastal residents, showed a huge umbrella
spread over Seattle's Space Needle, with the notation, "Give us your pale,
drenched, puddled masses."

Today's Tri-Cities offer a variety of amenities in addition to sunshine. Many
of these amenities were developed after World War II when rapid growth
brought on by nuclear energy and irrigation development left community
needs lagging.

Summer recreation in the Tri-Cities area focused around water sports on the local rivers. The Pasco Water Follies began after World War II when the first boat races took place on the Snake River near Sacajawea State Park. Other communities sponsored different events like fishing contests and regattas. Courtesy, Ralph Smith

Among the assets offered by the Tri-Cities are tourist facilities, new and improved hospitals, many choices in churches, and a variety of cultural events. Other aids to better living include an increasing array of upper-level educational courses, good libraries, senior citizen centers and retirement homes, and a wide selection of outdoor recreational opportunities.

A major result of all this has been a more stabilized community—a striking change from the transient mood that prevailed frequently in the late 1940s, 1950s, and 1960s. During these three decades, the presence of a huge proportion of newcomers, coupled with the lack of many desirable features of long-established communities, contributed to an irritating instability.

Today Tri-Cities residents not only feel much more at home, they also view

▲ ▲ ▲

Although most women no longer wear fur coats to shop, and the trees have been removed since this photograph was taken in 1944, this building on the corner of Lee Boulevard and George Washington Way continues to anchor Richland's downtown area as it has for nearly 70 years. Courtesy, Robley L. Johnson

their community as one that offers diversions for tourists, especially those preferring a leisurely, outdoor lifestyle. More than 2,000 motel rooms now are available for visitors. Teeing off at any one of seven golf courses offers a pleasant way to soak in the sunshine. Boating, fishing, cultural events, celebrations, and visits to museums and wineries are among other attractions.

The wineries—unanticipated two or three decades ago—now are scattered through the Tri-Cities vicinity, the neighboring Walla Walla area, and Yakima Valley. Chateau Ste. Michelle's $26-million Columbia Crest Winery at Paterson in southern Benton County is one of the Pacific Northwest's largest. One of the Tri-Cities' pioneers in the industry is Preston Wine Cellars north of Pasco, called the largest family-owned winery in the Northwest.

Also among tourist attractions are museums, which showcase the area's role in the nuclear industry and other phases of the past. One museum, the Hanford Science Center in the Federal Building in Richland, presents exhibits relating to the nuclear reservation. Visitors centers also are open near the Washington Public Power System's Plant 2 reactor and the Fast Flux Test Facility.

Displays of a more general historical type are presented at the old Pasco Carnegie Library in Pasco (by the Franklin County Historical Society), at the East Benton County Historical Society museum in Kennewick, the Benton County Museum in Prosser, and at Sacajawea Interpretive Center in Sacajawea

State Park, at the confluence of the Snake and the Columbia.

Many residents of the region own boats, especially since residents only have to travel a short distance to launch their craft on reservoirs developed behind Corps of Engineers' hydroelectric projects. The Corps has also provided parks, beaches, and boat launching areas along the Columbia and Snake rivers. The largest park in the Tri-Cities is the 430-acre Columbia Park at Kennewick, formerly operated by Benton County, but taken over in 1989 by the cities of Kennewick and Richland.

Fishing and bird hunting, always popular pastimes in the area, have been made more available from the development of irrigated agriculture in the first phase of the Columbia Basin Irrigation Project.

New reservoirs—and lakes formed by seepage—are now homes to thousands of ducks and geese, and a considerable percentage of these reservoirs are stocked with fish. The irrigation projects also have proven to be an ideal habitat for pheasants. The bird population has increased with annual plantings of pheasants from game farms. As a result the basin has been a sportsman's mecca during hunting and fishing seasons. The killing of pheasants and waterfowl rose sharply from the early 1950s to the mid-1960s, then began to decline.

Officials have attributed the diminishing population of wildlife to the lining of the canals' sides to reduce seepage, modern farming methods, the draining

▲ ▲ ▲

Listed on the National Register of Historic Places, the Moore Mansion began as part of the "model farm of the State of Washington" in 1908 and continued to be a showplace for a number of years. Its proximity to the Columbia River during prohibition made it a convenient nightclub. There was a concealed entry to the fourth-floor speakeasy, which accommodated about 70 spirited revelers. Courtesy, Franklin County Historical Society

▲ ▲ ▲

Built between 1912 and 1913, the Franklin County Courthouse with its stained glass dome and tiled rotunda, still graces Fourth Avenue in Pasco. Designed by the architectural firm of C. Lewis Wilson and company, the construction contract for $84,000 was awarded to Misho and Grant. Separate contracts provided the installation of light fixtures, plumbing fixtures, marblework, the glass dome, and two skylights. Courtesy, Franklin County Historical Society

of wetlands, and the use by farmers of pesticides, insecticides, and fertilizer. Federal and state officials are taking a closer look now at what needs to be done for habitat enhancement, in view of the experiences of the past several decades in the basin project.

"An ever-increasing population and continued development will no doubt mean an ever-shrinking base for wildlife," a Washington Department of Wildlife report commented. "At the same time, a growing human population will demand the quality and variety of wildlife recreation they have come to expect."

Efforts are under way to increase the number of migratory fish runs in the Columbia, Yakima, and Snake rivers that pass through the Tri-Cities. The buildup would affect the Ringold rearing facility for steelhead and salmon, located about 25 miles north of Pasco on the Columbia and operated by the departments of Fisheries and Wildlife. Further upstream, the Department of Fisheries manages a spawning channel at Priest Rapids Dam.

In the field of cultural activities, the Tri-Cities have a good selection, rating well for a community of its size. Several groups, such as the Mid-Columbia Symphony, the Richland Players, and the Richland Light Opera Company, date back to World War II or shortly thereafter. Most founders of the organizations either worked at the Hanford plant or were members of employees' families, who found diversions scarce and decided to make their own entertainment.

The Mid-Columbia Symphony Society has an orchestra of around 60 members and a youth symphony of nearly the same size, and sponsors a Young Artists competition that attracts some of the best young Columbia Basin musicians each year.

The symphony has provided music for other Tri-Cities groups, including the Mid-Columbia Regional Ballet and the Columbia Chorale, and has performed

▲ ▲ ▲
ABOVE: A testament to the technology of modern engineering, the Cable Bridge spans the mighty Columbia River, connecting the city of Pasco with the cities of Kennewick and Richland. Photo by John Clement

▲ ▲ ▲
LEFT: Soft moonlight bathes Rattlesnake Ridge in the subtle hues of the untamed desert. Photo by John Clement

▲ ▲ ▲

ABOVE: Firmly established in the arid regions of the western United States, the hardy and adaptive chukar is an indigenous creature of the mid-Columbia region. Photo by John Clement

▲ ▲ ▲

RIGHT: A southern exposure and many frost-free days make the Wahluke Slope north of Hanford an ideal location for the area's fruit crops. Here, luscious apricots ripen in the sun's warm glow. Photo by John Clement

▲ ▲ ▲

ABOVE: A dusting of autumn color highlights the desert floor along the banks of the Columbia River. Photo by John Clement

▲ ▲ ▲

LEFT: The smell of popcorn, and delighted squeals from the Ferris wheel add to the electric atmosphere of the Benton-Franklin County Fair. Photo by Harold Pleasant

▲ ▲ ▲

ABOVE: Rising in northwest Idaho and some 140 miles in length, the Palouse River flows west across the Washington border and empties into the Snake on the east border of Franklin County. The majestic Palouse River Canyon, pictured here, is located at Palouse Falls State Park—just about an hour's drive from the Tri-Cities vicinity. Photo by John Clement

▲ ▲ ▲

RIGHT: The Yakima River meets the Columbia River in a blazing sunrise near Bateman Island. Photo by John Clement

▲ ▲ ▲

ABOVE: Springtime bursts into color throughout the Horse Heaven Hills. Photo by John Clement

▲ ▲ ▲

LEFT: Potato production ranks high in the mid-Columbia agricultural community, illustrated by the sight of vast potato fields such as this one located north of Pasco. Photo by John Clement

▲ ▲ ▲

RIGHT: Rowing teams from the University of Washington, Oregon State, Washington State University, University of Southern California, and the University of California at Los Angeles race on the Columbia River during the Intercollegiate Sports Festival each year. Photo by John Clement

▲ ▲ ▲

ABOVE: Fishing has always been a favorite outdoor activity in the Tri-Cities area, encouraged by the myriad of waterways and reservoirs stocked with an abundant supply of gamefish. Photo by John Clement

▲ ▲ ▲

ABOVE: A local farmer proudly displays her bumper crop of delicious baby onions. Photo by John Clement

▲ ▲ ▲

LEFT: The annual Sunfest celebration is a favorite Tri-Cities festivity that features the music of the Mid-Columbia Symphony. Pictured here is a recent Sunfest audience. Photo by John Clement

▲ ▲ ▲

RIGHT: The Tri-Cities region is an important dryland wheat growing area with more than 300,000 acres dedicated to the crop in Benton and Franklin counties. Photo by John Clement

▲ ▲ ▲

BELOW: Much of the recreation in the Tri-Cities is centered around water sports and the use of the many parks, beaches, and launch areas constructed by the Corps of Engineers along the Snake and Columbia rivers. Photo by Harold Pleasant

during the annual Sunfest celebration. Symphony players also may be found in the orchestra pit for one of the Richland Light Opera's semiannual productions.

Ticket sales, grants from the Washington Commission for the Humanities and other art-related organizations, and corporate aid all help support the symphony's activities.

The annual concert season at Richland High School includes four concerts with guest artists, and a spring program featuring the top two winners of the Young Artists competition.

The Richland Light Opera Company (RLOC) had used Chief Joseph Junior High School auditorium in Richland for many years, and after that school's closure began using auditoriums in two high schools—Hanford and Richland. The group's auditions have attracted musicians, actors, dancers, and singers from a wide area. Many productions have been staged from Gilbert and Sullivan; one of RLOC's founders, Jack Quinn, was a Gilbert and Sullivan fan. A variety of more modern musicals also have been staged. Two shows are presented annually.

The Richland Players, formerly known as the Richland Village Players, have occupied a former movie theater—the Richland Theater on the Parkway— since 1971. They had performed earlier in Richland High School auditorium and the Village Theater. This group offers a wide selection of comedy, drama, and mystery, plus a children's show during the Christmas season. Volunteers build sets; borrow props from local stores, antique shops, and area homes; and sew and borrow costumes.

Several other newer organizations also have presented occasional productions in recent years in the Tri-Cities.

Dancing has also been a popular pastime in the region. One early group was the Dancers Guild in Richland, organized in the early 1950s. The Mid-Columbia Regional Ballet, founded in 1976, has made *The Nutcracker* a holiday tradition, has presented guest artists, and has brought in guest choreographers.

The Allied Arts Association, organized at Richland shortly after World War II,

▲ ▲ ▲
During early training flights in the early 1940s, teams of Navy pilots practiced landing on circle targets displayed on what became the Hanford Reservation. Here, planes are shown flying over what is now the Hanford Reach—the last free-flowing stretch of the Columbia River. Courtesy, Ralph Smith

▲ ▲ ▲

On February 11, 1944, painters put finishing touches on the first of two theaters built in Richland by the government to provide entertainment for the construction workers, scientists, and engineers at Hanford. These movie theaters were run by Midstate Amusement Company. In 1971 this building became the home of the Richland Players—an amateur theater group that currently provides a diverse program of drama and entertainment, marshalling talent and audiences from throughout the mid-Columbia region. Courtesy, Hanford Science Center

has brought local artists together. The association's annual sidewalk sale at Howard Amon Park has been a popular event, as has their more recent Sunfest celebrations. Beaux Arts, organized in the 1950s, mainly by Kennewick residents, sponsors an annual show at the Columbia Center shopping mall.

Annual celebrations and other events draw large crowds. Probably the most widely known is the Water Follies, highlighted by the unlimited hydroplane races for the Columbia Cup, on the Columbia River. The Sunfest is scheduled on summer weekends in Richland, featuring music festivals, arts and crafts, food booths, and other attractions. The Benton-Franklin Fair at Kennewick and Autumnfest at Pasco are among other annual events.

In the sports category, Tri-Cities residents have enjoyed minor-league baseball during many of the post-World War II years. The team has carried names such as the Braves, Imperials, Padres, and Triplets, and the management has changed frequently. From 1962 to 1971 the Tri-Cities team won several Northwest League championships. The most recent team, called the Triplets, won a league championship in 1984 before the franchise moved to Boise, Idaho, in 1987.

Ice Hockey is the newest professional sport available in the area. The new 6,000-seat coliseum at Kennewick is home to the Tri-City Americans, who compete in the Western Hockey League.

Continental Sports Corp. built the coliseum. The Americans played 17 games on the road before the building at Kennewick was ready. Ice hockey fans had bought 3,000 advance season tickets in one month, despite knowing little about the sport. A writer commented on early games: "Each game is a huge pep rally: the arena is festooned with homemade banners, a high school band leading the charge. The team hired local ethnic restaurants as concessionaires, making the Tri-Cities the only rink in the country to serve gyros, Mongolian beef and chicken enchiladas."

A short time after it opened in November 1988, the coliseum was made available for other events; nationally known entertainers began performing there. Previously, the Tri-Cities had no adequate facility for such shows.

High school athletic games have been a popular focus of local interest. One of the most notable coaching achievements in the high school field was chalked up by Art Dawald at Richland. His basketball teams were perennial strong contenders at state tournaments, and the subject of a book, *Bomber Mania*, by Ernest Jensen and Richard Swanson, covering the years 1953 to

1980. The writers became Bomber fans after starting to attend tournaments in the 1950s; they were Seattle residents at the time. "Nowhere has the combination of success on the court and unabashed fan enthusiasm reached such a high level as in the Atomic City," the writers claimed.

The media also has been a major contributor to the style of life in the Tri-Cities. Weekly newspapers were printed first, then radio stations and daily newspapers arrived on the scene. In recent years, television has had a big role in entertainment and news.

The Tri-City Herald, owned by McClatchy Newspapers of Sacramento, California, has been the community's only newspaper for more than a quarter of a century. After reaching nearly a 40,000 circulation in WPPSS construction days, the paper dropped back to about 33,000 daily, except for 36,000 on Sundays.

Herald editors have crusaded frequently for more coordination between communities and have favored consolidation of the three incorporated cities—but this issue lost consistently at the polls, the last time in 1988. The *Herald* was an ardent promoter of peacetime nuclear development in earlier years, and for a long time has strongly backed diversification of the economy, instead of relying solely on Hanford.

Scott Publishing Company was the original owner of *The Tri-City Herald*. The company purchased the weekly *Pasco Herald*, which started daily publication under the name of *The Tri-City Herald* in late 1947 with Glenn C. Lee, Hugh Scott, and Bob Philip in charge.

The Columbia Basin News, another daily, was established at Pasco in 1950, after the *Herald* moved to Kennewick. The *CBN*, as it was usually called, was a merger of two weeklies, *The Richland Villager* and *The Pasco News*. Howard Parish of Seattle was *CBN* publisher during most of the paper's life. Following a lengthy and often bitter battle between the two papers, complete with picketing, an antitrust suit, and numerous editorial attacks, the *CBN* folded in 1963.

Donald Pugnetti was the *Herald's* managing editor from 1947 to 1973, when he left to take the position of *Tacoma News-Tribune* editor. In 1979 publisher Glenn C. Lee cited age, health, and the expense of upgrading *Herald* equipment and office space as reasons for selling to the McClatchy chain.

Tri-Cities radio stations have reported fast-breaking news events and have

▲ ▲ ▲

In the 1960s the Tri-Cities Water Follies festivities included a beauty pageant complete with evening gown, bathing suit, and talent competitions. The winner presided over a variety of local events including a parade and boat races. Pictured here is Wendy Horrobin, crowned "Miss Tri-Cities" in 1969. She posed with a hydroplane on her head and with her hair styled to represent the rooster tail of spray caused by the rapid speed of the boats in the popular local races. Courtesy, Ralph Smith

▲ ▲ ▲

From 1950 until 1962 the Tri-City Braves entertained baseball fans at Sanders-Jacobs Field in the Kennewick Highlands near Morain and Clearwater avenues. More than 90,000 spectators attended games during the first season. Courtesy, East Benton County Historical Society

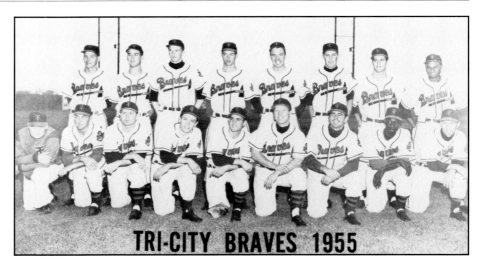

TRI-CITY BRAVES 1955

reflected changing musical tastes of the various eras. Sporting events have been broadcast in detail, and talk shows and religious programs have been among other radio fare.

The Tri-Cities' oldest station is KTCR (AM), owned by I-82 Acquisitions of Boise, Idaho. This was known as KPKW in 1945 when the station was established in two converted grain bins at Pasco. The P stood for Pasco, K for Kennewick, and W for Washington. Later, the call letters were changed to KGRS, KSMK, KOTY, and finally to KTCR (K Tri-Cities Radio). The FM station, still known as KOTY in 1990, dates to 1977.

Station KWIE, launched about 1948, was known later as KEPR, then KONA. These last letters were taken from a former Hawaiian station. KONA (FM) was established in 1969. Lloyd Aman, one of the Tri-Cities' most durable radio personalities, is an employee at KONA, which is owned by Tri-Cities Communications, Inc. KALE (AM), now owned by Sterling Recreation with KIOK (FM), dates from 1950. The FM station was started about 1978.

Several other stations also broadcast from the Tri-Cities and from Prosser.

Black and white television arrived in the 1950s, and in the 1960s presented vivid scenes of riots by blacks, protests against the Vietnam War, and combat scenes from southeast Asia. The medium has played an increasing role in news and entertainment, interspersed with its advertising messages.

The pioneering television station was KEPR of Pasco, Channel 19, which started in 1954 and is now a property of Retlaw Enterprises, Inc. Retlaw, owned by Walt Disney's widow Lillian and her two daughters, bought KEPR in 1986 from John Noel, Sr., and his son Rodger. Retlaw is Walter (for Walt Disney) spelled backwards. The rising value of such media properties is indicated by the $17 million paid by Retlaw for KEPR and stations KIMA of Yakima and KLEW in Lewiston.

Columbia Empire Broadcasting Corporation operates KNDU, Channel 25,

Kennewick, and KNDO, Yakima. Farragut Communications, Inc., purchased the stations in 1988 from Hugh Davis. KNDU, which dates from 1961, is affiliated with NBC, and KEPR is affiliated with CBS.

Kennewick's KVEW, Channel 42, established in 1970, is part of Apple Valley Broadcasting, Inc., along with station KAPP, Yakima. Apple is a subsidiary of Morgan Murphy Stations.

Public Broadcasting programs are shown on KTNW, Channel 31, a satellite of KWSU-TV of Pullman. This station has a local broadcasting staff, and may be housed in the future on the Washington State University branch campus at Richland. KTNW has a transmission tower at Jump Off Joe Butte near Kennewick.

The Tri-Cities' cable television franchise goes back to 1951, and cable now has a big following. Columbia Cable, owned by United Artists Cablesystems Corp., has operated the system since 1984.

Education is another field of activity that is important to a well-rounded lifestyle. In the Tri-Cities, elementary and secondary schools sometimes were overrun by children in earlier boom years, but construction programs and shifting populations have evened out each school's attendance, so that overcrowding is no longer a problem.

In higher education, Washington State University (WSU) recently chose Richland as the new home for a branch.

Establishment of the new campus is part of an effort overseen by the state's Higher Education Coordinating Board (HECB) to bring more educational programs to growing areas. Spokane, Vancouver, the Tri-Cities, and Puget Sound areas were listed where more college emphasis was required. WSU was given the responsibility to establish upper-division and graduate programs in the Tri-Cities.

"When one institution is responsible for a designated urban area, better service results," HECB noted. "One institution can respond more rapidly, provide greater continuity, and increase accountability."

Washington State University in the Tri-Cities area opened July 1, 1989, at Richland facilities that had been known as Tri-Cities University Center (TUC). The WSU branch campus, with 1,000 enrollment, offers undergraduate and graduate programs in science, engineering, general studies, and education. The new school is planning to open an $11.7 million addition in the fall of 1991.

The TUC had been sponsored by WSU,

▲ ▲ ▲
Picturesque Columbia Park is an ideal spot for taking a moment to feed the ducks and to enjoy a bit of outdoor recreation. Photo by Harold Pleasant

Local television and radio stations provide national news and cover local events such as the Benton-Franklin County Fair pictured here. Children throughout the two counties bring their animals to the fair to earn ribbons and money in the livestock auction. A strong 4-H program provides volunteers for the fair and opportunities for children to learn about livestock, agriculture, and homemaking. Courtesy, **Tri-City Herald**

which was responsible for financing; Eastern Washington University; and Central Washington University.

The school was an outgrowth of a nuclear engineering school operated by General Electric Co. when that firm was Hanford's main contractor. In the 1950s, several universities agreed to sponsor the educational programs. Sponsors have changed occasionally at TUC, which was known previously as the Joint Center for Graduate Study.

The Tri-Cities' largest upper-division school is Columbia Basin College (CBC), with about 5,500 full-time and part-time students. Most are working towards a two-year associate degree, college transfer credits, or vocational training.

CBC is well known for cultural programs and acts as sponsor for one of the Pacific Northwest's largest junior and senior high school jazz festivals. Music concerts, drama department outreach programs, and a town hall lecture series also add much interest for students and other area residents. CBC's athletics program attracts talented competitors from high schools around the Northwest.

CBC traces its start to 1946, when the Pasco School District began offering vocational and technical classes in buildings at the old Pasco Naval Air Station, under Jack Cooney's direction. In 1955 the State Board of Education approved Pasco as a junior college with the understanding that classes would be moved out of the old naval station as soon as possible.

The district received title to more than 150 acres at the present CBC site in 1956 and broke ground that year. In the next several years, the college expanded rapidly. Forty-three students graduated in the first class in 1957; the two receiving top honors were more than 40 years old.

Jack Cooney headed the college as director until 1962. Dr. Ronald Rippey was president from 1962 to 1965, followed by Dr. Lewis Ferrari, who served as acting president from 1965 to 1966, and Dr. Fred Esvelt, president from 1966 to December 1987. Dr. Marvin Weiss took over as president in February 1988.

In addition to public school systems, the Tri-Cities supports several parochial schools.

The oldest is Bethlehem Lutheran School sponsored by the Bethlehem Lutheran Church of Kennewick. The school history dates back to the Christian Day School founded in 1909.

▲ ▲ ▲

The Columbia Basin College campus soon included space for more classrooms, a library, music facilities, a gymnasium, administrative offices, and science and agricultural laboratories. Here, several students advise Dr. Ronald Rippey, the college's second president, on the best way to dig a planting hole in front of the Administration Building in 1963. Courtesy, Columbia Basin College

Numerous Catholics were among the people arriving in the Tri-Cities in the 1940s, and they soon wanted their own schools. St. Patrick's Catholic School of Pasco was started in 1951 and offers education through the sixth grade. Christ the King Catholic School of Richland (established in 1954) and St. Joseph Catholic School (started in Kennewick in 1964) provide classes through the eighth grade.

Tri-Citians also take pride in their libraries, all in modern buildings and well stocked with books. One of the most unusual in the Northwest is the Hanford Technical Library at Hanford, managed by Battelle Northwest. This library, established about 1948, contains around 27,000 books and 45,000 volumes of periodicals on scientific and technical subjects.

The Villagers, Inc., a group of local residents, started a library at Richland, then donated the books to General Electric Company for use in a community library. This group was established as a volunteer organization to provide some of the things that would not otherwise be available to this government-owned community. Later the incorporated city took over the facility.

Mid-Columbia Library manages libraries at Pasco, Kennewick, Connell, Benton City, and other outlying communities. Libraries have been established, too, at Columbia Basin College and the Tri-Cities Universities Center.

Churches also play a major role; the Tri-Cities Industrial Development Council reported more than 160 in the area.

One of the most novel is the United Protestant Church of Richland. This is an outgrowth of a Corps of Engineers policy during World War II. The Corps did not want to construct a building for every denomination, but agreed to provide one for the Catholics and another for Protestants. Richland's Protestant congregation liked the arrangement so well that it was continued after the war.

▲ ▲ ▲

Continuing education has always been a large part of Columbia Basin College's contribution to the mid-Columbia region. Two teachers are shown here dissecting goldfish during the third Radiation Workshop in February 1962 under the supervision of Columbia's instructors. Junior and senior high school teachers learned to use radiation monitoring equipment, testing for radioactive phosphorus. From left to right are geology instructor Stan White, Matthew Block, White Swan, Earl Pfeiffer, and chemistry instructor Warren Bartanen. Courtesy, Columbia Basin College

Central, the largest United Protestant church, has more than 3,000 members, three pastors, and five weekend services. This is sponsored by the United Methodist Church, and four other denominations each sponsor one of the four United Protestant churches in the Richland area—Westside, Northwest, Southside, and Bethany. In earlier years, more than a dozen denominations sponsored the United Protestant churches.

Tri-Cities' hospital bed count totals around 365, including a 24-bed substance abuse service unit at Our Lady of Lourdes Health Center in Pasco. The nonprofit Our Lady of Lourdes, which nearly doubled its size with an addition in the early 1980s, was the area's only hospital before World War II; it dates to 1916. Sisters of St. Joseph of Carondolet operate the Carondolet Regional Health System, which manages Our Lady of Lourdes and the Carondolet Psychiatric Care Center in Richland. Our Lady of Lourdes Hospital officials signed an agreement in 1987 to operate the 32-bed Mid-Columbia Mental Health Center, and in 1988 the name was changed to Carondolet Psychiatric Care Center.

Kennewick General Hospital, opened in 1952, is a general medical and surgical hospital, operated by a hospital district. Kadlec Medical Center, managed by a nonprofit hospital, formerly was supervised by the Methodist Church. It is named for Lieutenant Colonel Harry Kadlec, a Manhattan Engineer District officer who died on the Hanford job in World War II. Among this hospital's facilities is a neonatal intensive care unit (NICU).

In Pasco, La Clinica offers medical, dental, and mental health assistance. Among these are many Spanish-speaking migrant workers who help with the farm harvest in central Washington. In 1989, La Clinica received a $20,000 grant from Paul Newman's Salad King, Inc., to purchase a new van to bring children and families from outlying areas to Pasco for treatment.

A group with special interest in the continued development of good medical facilities is the senior citizen population, increasing here in ratio to the general populace, as elsewhere in the nation.

Each city has a senior citizens center serving daily lunches and sponsoring many events. The center in Richland is named for Harry Kramer, a community leader. Benton-Franklin Council on Aging, which manages the Richland center, has a contract for providing lunches five days a week from a Richland kitchen to the three centers. The council also is in charge of "meals on wheels" and other programs.

Private retirement complexes containing many units have been constructed for Tri-Cities' senior citizens. Some older residents also occupy quarters operated by housing authorities.

Pasco and Kennewick housing authorities have a lively history going back to World War II, when they provided temporary shelter for workers and their families, in government-approved facilities. Wartime units were removed, but more housing was constructed in later boom periods for low-income persons, many of whom are senior citizens. Parkside Homes in Pasco are basically for senior citizens, and a Kennewick highrise, Keewaydin Plaza, also houses senior citizens.

The Richland Housing Authority, established in 1981, has not built any housing units, but has acted as a landlord and retirement center manager.

In private housing, the most notable change in the past two decades has been the addition of apartments. Many were constructed in the 1970s, especially in and near fast-growing Kennewick. While many apartment residents represent the more mobile segment of the population, the units are a long way in style from the temporary quarters of the early boom era, when thousands of trailers became a prime symbol of the tendency to move in and out on a short notice. The development of an established community has been a major achievement.

As one of the larger urban centers in a state ranking unusually high in population growth, the Tri-Cities anticipate sharing in the continued influx of new enterprises and residents. These changes are foreshadowed by large growth in western Washington state in 1990 in the Seattle metropolitan area, although Tri-Cities leaders are planning for a more gradual transition that will ensure the area retains its present amenities while accommodating population increases.

▲ ▲ ▲

Construction of two Richland churches was completed in time for Christmas Eve services in 1944. The pastor of the United Protestant Church, pictured here upon its completion, was Dr. Thomas Acheson. Father William J. Sweeney presided at the Catholic church, which had a similar floor plan but no steeple. Courtesy, Hanford Science Center

Partners in Progress

▲ ▲ ▲

S peeding toward the year 2000, the Tri-Cities is poised to become Washington state's "city of the 1990s." In a time when many communities are facing runaway growth, lack of urban planning, pollution of the land and water, inadequate schools, and reliance on single industries, the Tri-Cities stands out as a model for the future.

The companies who have chosen to be profiled in this section are a testament to the commitment of Tri-Citians to create a quality environment for work and play. The diverse companies have a common thread—an ability to grow and change with the needs of the community.

At the turn of the century what are now known as Kennewick, Pasco, and Richland were little more than a few small farm communities. For more than four decades the Tri-Cities' existence was based on serving an agricultural economy.

During World War II the face of these rural communities in southeastern Washington, as well as the world as a whole, would be forever changed. Scientists in Europe were uncovering the secrets of a new science—the atom. In the early 1940s, 600 square miles along the Columbia River was chosen as the location for a primary site of the Manhattan Project.

Literally overnight, a combined population of 6,000 people grew to more than 56,000. People were recruited nationwide for the "Hanford

Works." It was such a top-secret project, that most employees did not know what they were working on, only that it would help end the war.

The sudden growth in population leveled off at the close of the war. The government, however, had assumed the role of a global power, and, as a result, Hanford continued to operate. Yet government funding during the next 40 years would be politically driven, and the Tri-Cities' economy would become cyclical.

During the 1950s the agricultural community was dramatically impacted by the government's project to construct dams on the Columbia River, resulting in hundreds of thousands of acres of land becoming irrigated. Dryland farm crops were joined by or substituted with higher-value irrigated farm crops.

▲ ▲ ▲

Clad in the sporting equipment of the day, Kennewick High School's first football team gathered for a studio portrait in 1909. Looking barely older than the players, Coach Horace E. Groom (back row, left) and Superintendent Melvin Lewis (back row, right), posed with their team. Nicknames were popular in 1909 and this team included a "Tubby," "Brick," "Tink," "Babe," and "Pinkie." Courtesy, East Benton County Historical Society

As the Tri-Cities entered the 1980s, the political and business environments were undergoing tremendous changes. Grain embargos had a tremendous impact on the farm community. The political arena had changed, and the mission at Hanford was in question. Local businesses were experiencing consistently low sales. Each city began to aggressively pursue business opportunities and to communicate the message that the Tri-Cities was a good place for business.

An aggressive program of economy diversification was also developed in 1988. This plan was to be carried forward by the Tri-City Industrial Development Council (TRIDEC), an organization that had its roots several decades before in ensuring the continued funding of Hanford.

The recent years have been a time of challenge and opportunity for the Tri-Cities, and the results are beginning to show. Some of the Tri-Cities success stories include an expanded shopping mall, a new coliseum seating 6,000 people, state-of-the-art hospitals in all three cities, the Tri-Cities airport expansion, the growth of local winemaking, the variety of 60 different agricultural crops, investors from the Pacific Rim and Europe, a new local branch of Washington State University, and Hanford, creating a new mission with centers of excellence in molecular research, technology transfer, and environmental cleanup. The Tri-Cities is poised and ready to be the model for community development in the twenty-first century.

Tri-City Industrial Development Council

Tri-City Industrial Development Council's vision statement says, "In the year 2000, the image of the Tri-Cities is based on the three tiers of technology, agriculture, and health and leisure. Environmental degradation and overcrowding in the central Puget Sound area has driven growth to Eastern Washington. The Tri-Cities has emerged as a growth center, a community with a vibrant populace, with a vision of a preferred future, built on enormous pride and energy, all developed after many years of struggle. The image of the Tri-Cities reflects its people and their attitude, never looking back, always moving forward."

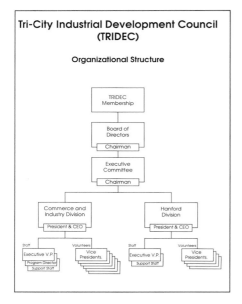

The development of the vision statement in 1988 was the result of more than 250 Tri-Citians, representing a cross-section of backgrounds, joining the members and staff of the Tri-City Industrial Development Council (TRIDEC) to create a master plan for the Tri-Cities' entrance into the twenty-first century. The plan was named "Renaissance."

TRIDEC is the area's economic development and lobbying organiza-

tion, which itself has grown and evolved during several decades to respond to the changing needs of the community. The organization was created in the early 1960s under another name, the Tri-City Nuclear Industrial Council, to protect the Hanford Site, a federal government defense installation, from congressional budget cuts. The site was the area's major employer.

In 1985 the organization was

renamed the Tri-City Industrial Development Council (TRIDEC), and its role was expanded to include local economic development and diversification as a part of Governor Booth Gardner's "Team Washington" initiative. That same year TRIDEC expanded again when it acquired the Tri-Cities Chamber of Commerce. In 1986 a managing director was hired to create a wide-ranging economic development program for the Tri-Cities. Two years later two major Hanford programs were cut from the federal budget resulting in substantial local layoffs. The federal, state, and local governments, and, most important, local businesses all stepped in to save the local economy.

The Renaissance team raised $2.3 million to implement the master plan. The state also contributed di-

versification funding, and the federal government created a "loaned executive" program to provide professional staff to help facilitate TRIDEC's diversification programs. With this infusion of support, TRIDEC's staff was expanded in 1989 from four to 10 people, plus eight loaned executives. With an annual operating budget of $1.5 million, the program became the largest in the State of Washington.

By 1990 the Tri-Cities had suc-

▲ ▲ ▲
The Tri-City Industrial Development Council (TRIDEC) headquarters at 901 North Colorado in Kennewick.

ceeded in creating a framework for a new community image—one that projected a diverse business base, centers of excellence in research and technology transfer, commitment to a quality education system, a broad-based agricultural program, and an uncompromised quality of life. The challenge for the decade of the 1990s is to mobilize the community to make permanent these images. Tri-City Industrial Development Council is committed to that goal, so that when the Tri-Cities arrives at the year 2000, its residents will be living their vision, not by accident, but by choice.

American National Bank

In 1980, when the last independent bank in Benton County was sold, many Tri-City businesspeople expressed concern that local residents and small businesses would not continue to enjoy the banking services they were used to. In response to this concern, a group of area investors organized and began the task of opening a new, locally owned and operated bank. The group consisted of Russell J. Dean, Craig Eerkes, Richard C. Emery, Harvey Faurholt, George A. Grant, Robert R. Matheson, E. Neal Smiley, Joe G. Vincent, E.A. "Pete" White, William E. Wright, and George Yoshino. In a short time they raised the capital to finance a bank, fulfilled regulatory requirements necessary to operate a bank, and hired staff from the local community to manage a bank.

On October 25, 1982, American National Bank (ANB) opened at 7525 Canal Drive in Kennewick under the management of Richard C. Emery (now chief executive officer and president) and Lowell H. Davis (now vice president and cashier). American National Bank's management believed there was a need to provide local consumers with more personalized service at all levels and was the first bank to offer extended hours at drive-up windows.

American National Bank management also instituted a practice of ensuring that all bank staff were readily accessible to depositors and began a concerted effort to support smaller operations and leave the national and multinational companies to the larger banks. Borrowers as well as depositors could feel confident that their money was being invested in the Tri-Cities.

American National Bank has enjoyed a growth rate of 11 percent to 40 percent annually since 1982 and has received an "A" rating, which in the banking industry makes it one of the safest and soundest institutions in the nation. Even though the Tri-Cities have experienced economic swings during the past several years, the community has continued to support the bank. In 1985, as a result of the institution's steady growth and success, a new branch office was opened in downtown Kennewick. In 1988 the West Richland branch was added. American National Bank is the only bank doing business in Benton County with its headquarters in the state of Washington.

American National Bank is a member of the Washington Bankers Association, the American Institute of Banking, and the Independent Bankers Association of America. The bank's employees are actively involved in local professional and civic organizations. In 1988 ANB began sponsoring the American National Bank Cougar Golf Classic to raise money for Washington State University.

A staff of seven people has

▲ ▲ ▲
The current trend in banking of extended hours has been a standard practice at American National Bank. From the very start in 1982, ANB has been open from 8 a.m. to 7 p.m. during the week and from 9:30 a.m. to 5 p.m. on Saturday.

grown to its current 26 employees. President Richard Emery believes the resources available in the three communities are unique, and ANB will be responsive to the Tri-Cities' growth and diversification. As an active team player, American National Bank will continue to lead the local banking industry in providing the banking services needed to meet the challenges facing the area.

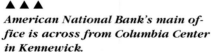

▲ ▲ ▲
American National Bank's main office is across from Columbia Center in Kennewick.

George A. Grant, Inc.

It was 1936. George A. Grant was a mechanical engineering student at Washington State University. He was determined to work on what promised to be one of the most important engineering feats of the century. Grant was not about to miss the opportunity of a lifetime.

The Columbia Basin Project, as it was known, would take more than three decades to complete. The focal point of the project was the Bureau of Reclamation's construction of the Grand Coulee Dam. Grant joined more than 2,000 other young engineers and construction workers, and from 1936 to 1941 he worked as an engineer on the dam. In 1938 he married his sweetheart Marianne, and they have recently celebrated their 50th wedding anniversary, hosted by their six children. Grant served in the Army for five years and in 1946 fin-

ished his tour of duty as a lieutenant colonel. He remained in the Army reserves and is now a retired colonel in the Corps of Engineers.

After the war Grant returned to the Bureau of Reclamation and worked on the Columbia Basin Project for two more years. In 1948 he moved his family to Pasco, and for the next seven years he refined his engineering skills working for two Tri-City construction companies.

In 1955, with the support of his wife and friends, Grant started his own construction firm out of his home in Pasco. The business prospered, and two years later he moved the operation to his current location in Richland and named it George A. Grant, Inc. His office, shop, equipment yard, and other business facilities are part of a 20-acre complex along Wellsian Way, including the World War II quonset hut that served as George's first corporate office.

Over the past 30 years the firm has constructed more than $150 million in facilities at Hanford, including

▲ ▲ ▲
George and Marianne Grant on the occasion of their 50th wedding anniversary.

projects in the 100, 200, 300, and 400 areas; Washington Public Power supply system projects 1, 2, and 4; the Exxon nuclear complex (now ANF); and part of the buildings comprising the Battelle Northwest Laboratories complex. These projects required mandatory high-level security clearances and the highest level of quality-assurance/quality-control programs.

In addition to projects at Hanford, the firm has performed work for the Corps of Engineers, including recreation facilities at Crow Butte State Park at the John Day Reservoir, railroad facilities on the Columbia and Snake rivers, fish protection facilities on the dams from John Day to Lower Granite on the Columbia and Snake rivers, and headgate structures on Libby Dam in Montana. The firm also performed work on Bureau of Reclamation projects such as the construction of irrigation facilities, underground drainage projects in the Columbia Basin (more than 100 miles), the bureau's administrative office at Grand Coulee, fish ladders on the Yakima

▲ ▲ ▲
FFTF Project 400 Area, DOE Hanford, 1980.

and Umatilla rivers, and filtration plants on the Okanogan River.

Grant's company did not stop at government construction projects. Locally it left its stamp on the Hanford House, HAPO Credit Union, Central United Protestant Church, Old National Bank, Sea-First Bank, St. Patrick's Church, Highland Shopping Center, Sandvik Special Metals manufacturing plant, Iowa Beef Processors packing plant, and Wendy's drive-in restaurants.

In addition to establishing a as a national director, and after 12 years as director, he was made lifetime national director. In 1989 Grant received the Skill-Integrity-Responsibility Award from the Inland Empire Chapter of the AGC. The award was only the fifth given in 65 years. He was one of the original board members of the Tri-City Nuclear

▲ ▲ ▲
The Hanford House Resort Building was constructed in 1968 by George A. Grant, Inc.

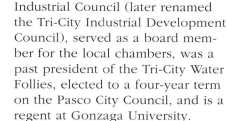

strong presence in the community as a businessman, Grant also took the time to become involved in several professional and civic organizations. In 1965 he joined the Associated General Contractors (AGC) Inland Empire Chapter and served as president in 1970. In 1972 he was elected

▲ ▲ ▲
The corporate officers include (from left) Barbara DeWitz, treasurer; Richard Richter, vice president; and Ron Grant, vice president.

▲ ▲ ▲
The Physician's Clinic in Pasco, a George A. Grant, Inc., construction project.

Industrial Council (later renamed the Tri-City Industrial Development Council), served as a board member for the local chambers, was a past president of the Tri-City Water Follies, elected to a four-year term on the Pasco City Council, and is a regent at Gonzaga University.

Grant attributes his success and longevity in the Tri-Cities to a fair and consistent approach to business, as well as providing a positive environment in the work place for his employees. His policies generated substantial repeat business that allowed the company to grow and increase staff. Grant has 15 to 25 full-time staff, along with an average of 50 hourly employees. During construction peaks, employment increases to more than 200 people.

Grant has experienced little turnover in more than 30 years of doing business. He still makes it a point to visit all company projects, but in the past few years has relied on his senior staff, including vice president Jay Alford, who recently retired after 24 years of service, and current vice presidents Richard Richter and Ron Grant. Former office managers Emma Pugh, Thelma Charles, and Arlene Hormel, and current office manager Barbara DeWitz have been responsible for assuring efficient office operations.

George A. Grant is not planning an early retirement. He and his staff at George A. Grant, Inc., will continue to take an active role in projects that will enhance the Tri-Cities diversification efforts.

Tri-City Herald

Volume 1, No. 1, of the first daily newspaper in the history of the Tri-Cities hit the streets on the afternoon of November 13, 1947. The *Tri-City Herald* was born from the *Pasco Herald,* a 10-page weekly with a circulation of 2,000 that had been acquired a month before by Glenn C. Lee and Robert Philip.

Since 1979 it has been part of McClatchy Newspapers, an organization rich in the history of American journalism. The company was born in 1857, when the *Sacramento Bee* was founded under the direction of James McClatchy. Today another James McClatchy, the company's publisher and chairman, and Erwin Potts, its chief executive officer, direct the firm from its headquarters in Sacramento, California.

The *Tri-City Herald* is managed for McClatchy by Kelso Gillenwater, only the third publisher in the history of the newspaper. Gillenwater has been publisher since 1981. He came to the Tri-Cities from Norfolk, Virginia, where he was president and chief operating officer of Landmark Community Publishing Company, which published large weekly and

▲▲▲
This is how the main Kennewick office looked in 1955 when growth had required the old cannery be expanded on the southeast to accommodate a rotary press bought from the **Minneapolis Star & Tribune.**

▲▲▲
Herald librarian Dori O'Neal maintains files of all locally written stories and all photographs that appear in the **Herald.**

small daily newspapers in six states. The managing editor is Jack Briggs, its fifth editor. Briggs began his career at the *Herald* in 1960 as a reporter and became managing editor in 1985.

The *Herald* is just the latest in a series of newspapers that have served the Tri-Cities since the 1880s. They include the *News-Recorder,* the *Columbia Courier,* the *Twin City Reporter,* the *Pasco Express,* the *Kennewick Courier-Reporter,* the *Benton County Advocate,* and the *Pasco Empire*—all weeklies.

For 13 years beginning in 1950 the *Herald* had competition from a second daily newspaper. The Pasco-based *Columbia Basin News* was subsidized by the International

▲▲▲
The **Tri-City Herald's** *editorial board comprises (from left) managing editor Jack Briggs, publisher Kelso Gillenwater, and editorial-page editor Matt Taylor.*

Typographical Union (ITU), which helped bankroll the *News* after the ITU became embroiled in a labor dispute with the *Herald.*

Over the years the *Herald* has gone from hot-type composition and letterpress printing to photo offset reproduction, from the hot snap of antique Underwood typewriters to the mellow click of computer terminals, from the buzz of wire machines spitting out news from the Associated Press to a satellite dish

▲ ▲ ▲
Herald *marketing director Jack Kelly and advertising saleswoman Micki Eby go over the details of an ad.*

shooting news from around the world into the *Herald's* computer room. These achievements were milestones in a history that was sometimes a battle for survival.

In the 1950s owners Lee and Philip sold subscriptions door to door to increase circulation and sold advertising by personally visiting local merchants. In those early years Lee sold personal possessions to pump cash into the business to keep it operating. With an editorial staff headed by editor Hugh Scott (and followed by Don Pugnetti and Bill Bequette), the owners of the new daily practiced aggressive advocacy

▲ ▲ ▲
ABOVE: The Herald building as it looks today—transformed by millions of dollars spent expanding the structure and transforming the news operation from days when national and international news trickled in by phone to now when it is captured by satellite dish (seen on the roof) at high speed.

journalism that always stirred interest and often controversy.

Today the newspaper is published in a newly remodeled facility at the corner of Cascade Street and Canal Drive in downtown Kennewick. The heart of the building remains the bankrupt cannery Lee bought with $40,000 of borrowed money when his efforts to keep the newspaper in Pasco failed after he bought the weekly.

In those early years as a daily, the *Herald* was sometimes a maker of the news. When the ITU struck

▲ ▲ ▲
BELOW: Clay Myers, head of Computer Services, and his assistant Lisa Farnham examine the working parts of one of the many computers that help run the **Tri-City Herald** *operations.*

▲ ▲ ▲
The remodeled Herald building's main entrance opens to the classified advertising and business departments, situated where the old rotary printing press used to be.

the newspaper, charging it was unfair to organized labor, Lee picketed the picketers for being what he considered unfair to the *Herald.* The newspaper, through Lee's "The Way I See It" column, became embroiled in 1951 in a controversy involving the Kennewick School District. It was this controversy that eventually led to the recall of the school board and libel suits against the *Herald,* some of which the paper lost and some of which it won. Later, when asked who came out ahead in the Kennewick school fight, Lee responded, "The Kennewick School District."

It was one of many battles the *Herald* would involve itself in over the years. Lee fought on the local, state, and national scenes through his newspaper for what he regarded as the economic betterment of the Tri-Cities.

An era passed

▲ ▲ ▲

Working on a light table, Margaret Malabnini positions advertisements for a page in the **Herald.**

in October 1979, when Glenn Lee announced he was selling the newspaper after 32 years as publisher. He became publisher emeritus, a title he held until his death on August 8, 1985.

McClatchy moved quickly to modernize and strengthen the *Herald,* reflecting the philosophy expressed by James McClatchy when he founded the first of several McClatchy newspapers more than 130 years ago: "The object of this newspaper is not only independence, but permanence."

To ensure and enhance that permanence, McClatchy invested heavily to modernize facilities and equipment.

A Saturday edition was added on September 5, 1981. Three years later, to make the news even more timely for readers, the *Herald* converted from afternoon to morning publication. Conversion to the morning cycle was an important national trend that was launched in the 1970s

▲ ▲ ▲

The **Herald** *has a newsroom staff of about 40 people, who work in a room that was remodeled as part of a million-dollar project in 1987.*

by McClatchy newspapers.

The *Herald*'s old press, built in 1928 and capable of producing 18,000

copies per hour, was replaced in 1982 with a press with the speed of 57,000 copies per hour and improved reproduction. In 1988 the *Herald* replaced that press with an offset press that allows for an even more attractive and readable paper. In 1989 the newspaper began expanding news coverage in the outlying region.

A million-dollar project in 1987 that rebuilt 18,000 square feet of the

▲ ▲ ▲

In 1949 the **Herald** *expanded by opening this "office" in the totally government-owned and -operated town of Richland. Office space was hard to find in those days.*

▲ ▲ ▲
Editors gather at 4 p.m. each day to discuss the day's top local, state, national, and international news stories and decide where in the following day's paper those top stories will be displayed.

most rapid growth and expansion.

In 1990 Gillenwater was named Tri-Citian of the Year, an honor bestowed on his predecessor, Glenn Lee, in 1980.

The *Herald's* challenge in the future is to maintain its local predominance while working to build more readership throughout the re-

60-year-old building reflects "our long-term faith in the community and in the Tri-Cities as a good environment in which to conduct our business," publisher Gillenwater says. These efforts are among the reasons that the *Herald* has one of the highest penetration rates of daily newspapers in the Northwest.

In the 1980s the *Herald* maintained its traditional role as a leader in community issues. During a decade of economic turbulence, the

newspaper actively pursued the creation of a new university campus in the Tri-Cities—a new branch of Washington State University—and also helped build the Tri-City Industrial Development Council (TRIDEC) into a major economic development force in the region. Gillenwater led that organization as chairman during its two years of

▲ ▲ ▲
In October 1948 the Tri-City Herald moved its printing plant from Pasco to the site of the bankrupt K&P Cannery in Kennewick. It is around this 1906 building that the many expansions of the Herald plant have taken place in downtown Kennewick.

▲ ▲ ▲
Computers have replaced the old typewriters in most every newsroom, including the Herald's. Here assistant managing editor Ken Robertson composes a news page on a special pagination computer.

gion, Gillenwater says. That will be accomplished by extending the paper's news-gathering strengths to communities that encircle the Tri-Cities, while retaining the high-quality news operation in its core area of Kennewick, Pasco, and Richland.

City Of Richland

Richland is a community where a sunny climate has been combined with a superior quality of life and a competitive business environment to produce an oasis of opportunity. The availability of affordable land, the presence of a skilled work force, the existence of a strong infrastructure and abundant power, and the presence of a modern transportation network (including rail, air, water, and interstate highway system) are just a few of the elements that have attracted people, businesses, and industries to Richland.

In an effort to continue to encourage new business ventures in the community, the City of Richland constructed the Horn Rapids Business Park. The focal point of the park is the Tri-Cities Enterprise Center, a business incubation facility providing the environment necessary for new businesses to grow and develop. Surrounding the center is competitively priced land for industrial utilization, with streets, lights, and utilities already in place. The business park provides a cost-effective alternative to industries wishing to build their future with a young, progressive community.

Richland's municipal government

▲ ▲ ▲
An aerial view of the Columbia Point Marina Park Project in Richland.

▲ ▲ ▲

Recreational activities at Richland's Howard Amon Park on the Columbia River.

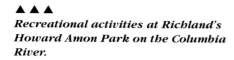

has built a community that preserves the integrity of neighborhoods and recreational areas. The city has invested heavily in the development of parks, beaches, and other water-oriented facilities that provide the ideal setting for boating, sailing, windsurfing, water skiing, running, bicycling, and other outdoor sports.

Richland plays host to a variety of outdoor events such as the Northwest Regional Rowing Regatta, the Western

Outboard Hydroplane Championships, the Northwest Classic Air Race, the Academy of Model Aeronautics National Championships, as well as other local and regional baseball, swimming, golf, and tennis tournaments.

Further development is under way to enhance land within the central core of the community along the Columbia River—an area that already contains a park, outdoor amphitheatre, hotel, golf course, and yacht club. It will include a mixed-

▲ ▲ ▲

ABOVE: Richland, with its sunny climate and ideal location along the Columbia River, welcomes individuals and business and industry seeking a better life in the state of Washington.

LEFT: The Tri-Cities Enterprise Center, located at Richland's Horn Rapids Business Park, provides the environment for new businesses to grow at a reasonable cost.

use project and a destination resort and conference center with accompanying restaurants and shops to further open the waterfront to residents and visitors.

The original town of Richland was incorporated in 1910. It was primarily an agricultural community, with a population in the early 1940s of less than 300 people. In 1943 the federal government selected the town and surrounding areas as the site for the construction of the country's first nuclear reactors. Richland was rebuilt to house the thousands of workers imported from all over the country to support the Hanford Atomic Works. The follow-up research and development in the 1950s was the precursor to the constructive utilization of nuclear energy.

Energy-related activities at Hanford have been and will continue to be a major element in the

overall economic success of Richland and its neighboring communities of Kennewick and Pasco. In 1958 the city was returned to the citizens and was incorporated as a first-class municipality in the State of Washington.

The most dynamic asset found in Richland are the people. The warmth and hospitality of local residents are

evident throughout the community. Richland continues to offer an outstretched hand to new businesses, industries, and residents looking for a superior quality of life in Washington and the Pacific Northwest.

▲ ▲ ▲

Columbia Point and Wellsian Way development areas adjacent to Interstate 182.

Kennewick General Hospital

Kennewick General Hospital (KGH) is a community hospital built upon the strong foundation of its past and poised to accept the challenges of the 1990s. With the completion of a $6.6-million renovation project in 1989, KGH continues its commitment to the community by providing excellence in medical care and utilization of state-of-the-art technology. The two-year renovation project focused on the construction of the Family Birthing Center, expanded emergency and surgery departments, a new intensive care and coronary care unit, an enlarged laboratory, a new drive-through front entrance, and enlarged cafeteria.

According to hospital staff, KGH has moved away from the cold,

▲ ▲ ▲

Kennewick General Hospital has recently undergone a $6.6-million remodeling project resulting in a state-of-the-art, 71-bed facility to serve the Tri-Cities.

▲ ▲ ▲

The new Jack Barnes Intensive Coronary Care Unit features a combination of custom-designed space, state-of-the-art equipment, and well-trained medical staff, all of which contribute to quality care of patients.

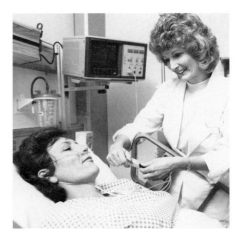

white, sterile atmosphere that dominated medical facilities for years, to a physical environment of soft pastels and neutral shades that reflect the caring, nurturing, and supportive environment that is found throughout KGH's corridors. A supportive patient environment only begins with the physical features of the hospital. Specialized facilities and services have been designed to respond to the changes in community needs.

KGH's Family Birthing Center is just one example of the hospital's commitment to the family. There are no labor and delivery rooms now. There are only birthing rooms, with ancillary equipment and support

systems within easy access. The Family Birthing Center encourages immediate bonding between not only the mother and newborn, but with other family members as well. KGH also offers prenatal, parenting, sibling, and grandparent classes. Specially trained nurses continue to give care 24 hours per day, even after mother and child leave for home. The nurses are as close as the telephone.

The intensive care and coronary

▲ ▲ ▲

The new KGH Family Birthing Center is the only facility in the area custom-designed to service the needs of the entire family during the birthing process.

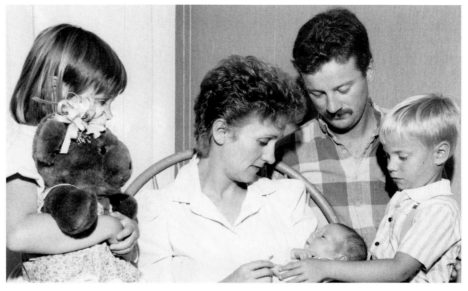

care unit for seriously ill patients is another example of the high degree of care available at KGH. The facility reflects a modular concept with a central nurses' station, computerized systems to monitor patients, and skilled staff. Staff in all phases of hospital operations and procedures are constantly upgrading their skills, with specialized educational programs and in-service training. The Emergency Department of KGH is the busiest in the Tri-Cities, seeing nearly 30,000 patients per year.

Another aspect of KGH's commitment is its relationship with Deaconess Medical Center's Lifebird and Sacred Heart Medical Center's Heartflite air-transport helicopters, which can move patients within minutes to specialized clinics and hospitals in Spokane and other large metropolitan areas.

Kennewick General Hospital was the first hospital to introduce a medically monitored weight-loss program. The Optifast program is the fastest growing weight-loss program in the country.

Kennewick General Hospital is also visible in community events. Hospital staff provide free first aid at the annual Columbia Cup hydroplane races. More than 45 specially trained volunteers operate three medical-aid areas. KGH also provides medical care for the Tri-City Americans hockey team and free first aid at the annual Benton/Franklin County Fair.

Kennewick General Hospital has its roots in the community. Kennewick residents began the drive for a local hospital in the late 1930s. By 1950 the fund-raising board was well on its way to raising the needed funds and was boosted in its efforts by a gift of $150,000 in surplus equipment from the Atomic Energy Commission. By 1951 a $350,000 bond was passed and construction began on the hospital.

One of the most important fund-raising groups was the KGH Auxiliary, a group of more than 200

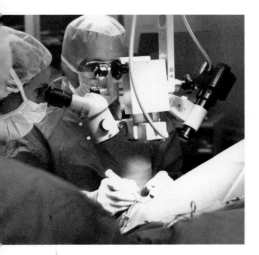

▲ ▲ ▲

At KGH, patients will not only receive excellent medical attention, but will discover that the staff really care.

women who worked on everything from sewing the curtains for the new hospital, to canning and donating as many as 1,000 quarts of fruits and vegetables in the first couple of years. The KGH auxiliary has worked for the hospital since it opened and is still working. The hospital's Foundation has also been very active on behalf of KGH.

The community's dream came true on July 26, 1952, when the 46-bed hospital opened. Throughout the 1950s the community continued its support of the hospital as it expanded the equipment and services offered. In the early 1960s a 12-bed pediatrics department opened to relieve the overcrowding. By 1967 excavation started on another addition that included a third operating room, additional beds, relocation of the obstetrical department, and an outpatient department. The expansion to 60 beds was completed in 1968, and at the present time KGH offers 71 beds. In 1985 KGH established the Columbia Center Clinic.

The Kennewick community had the foresight and faith to establish Kennewick General Hospital and has the devotion and commitment to keep it growing.

Washington Public Power Supply System

The Washington Public Power Supply System (Supply System) was organized in 1957 as a municipal corporation and joint operating agency of the State of Washington. The Supply System, with its headquarters in Richland, is empowered to acquire, construct, and operate facilities for the generation and transmission of electric power. The Supply System has 13 members—10 Public Utility Districts and the cities

▲ ▲ ▲
Supply System engineers are constantly upgrading plant systems to make it a more efficient power producer.

of Seattle, Tacoma, and Richland. The Supply System is committed to helping the Bonneville Power Administration maintain the region's low-cost electric rates through prudent management of the nuclear Plant 2 and the Packwood Lake Hydroelectric Project.

The 27.5-megawatt Packwood Project, located about 20 miles southeast of Mount Rainier, was the Supply System's first power-generating project. Construction began in 1962, and Packwood began operations in June 1964. It has produced more than 2.8 billion kilowatt-hours

▲ ▲ ▲
ABOVE: Refueling of Plant 2 occurs annually. More than 500 workers are hired locally for annual maintenance and refueling.

of electricity for the Bonneville Power Administration and the 12 utilities that financed its construction.

The Supply System also pioneered the generation of electricity using nuclear power. On September 26, 1963, President John F. Kennedy signed a bill that authorized the Atomic Energy Commission to sell by-product steam from the government's N-reactor to the Supply System. The Hanford Generating Project (HGP) was completed in 1966, with a capacity to produce 860 megawatts of power. The HGP operated until January 1987, when it was shut down because steam for the generation of electricity was no longer available from the N-reactor.

During the late 1960s regional power planners estimated that increased use of electric power

through the end of the century required the construction of numerous power-generating facilities. The Supply System began construction of five nuclear power generating facilities (WNP 1,2 3, 4, and 5). The Supply System's nuclear Plant 2 was officially declared in commercial operation on December 13, 1984. The Supply System's Projects 1 and 3 are near completion and on construction standby, while Projects 4 and 5 have been canceled.

Plant 2 became the state's first commercial nuclear power plant, generating 1,100 megawatts of electricity—enough to power Seattle. Electricity from Plant 2 is sold at cost to the federal Bonneville Power Administration and pooled with electricity produced by six other thermal

▲ ▲ ▲
Plant 2, Washington's only commercial nuclear power plant, started operating in 1984. The plant supplies enough electricity for a city of 500,000 people.

plants and 30 federal hydroelectric plants throughout the Northwest.

In all phases of Plant 2, concern for the environment and the public's health and safety has been paramount. Training programs ensure that Plant 2 workers have the necessary qualifications and skills to protect public safety through safe and reliable operation. Workers are trained in the areas of health physics and chemistry, maintenance, safety, fire protection, emergency procedures, and security.

A specially designed, state-of-the-art training facility located near Plant 2 contains sophisticated training aids, including a computerized control-room simulator. This simulator, a duplicate of the Plant 2 control room, allows operators to hone their skills in routine operating procedures and to learn to deal with

abnormal events and simulated accidents. Plant operators spend one week of every six in rigorous training, continually increasing their level of knowledge.

Supply System emergency planners share a common goal with the community: to protect the health and safety of the public. They work closely with local, state, and federal government agencies; law enforcement agencies; and community volunteer agencies to develop procedures to respond at any given time, on any day, and work as a team to effectively handle any emergency.

Supply system environmental scientists and biologists constantly monitor the rural area surrounding Plant 2. Environmental studies in the surrounding area are routinely conducted on milk and farm crop samples, soil, vegetation, water from the

nearby Columbia River, and aquatic and terrestrial animal life to make sure plant operations have minimal impact on the environment.

Public education is another commitment the Supply System has made to the local area. Staff from the Supply System work with students, tours of Supply System facilities are available, a speakers' bureau provides programs on request for interested groups, a wide variety of printed materials has been produced for public use, and the Supply System operates the Plant 2 Visitors' Center. Inside the center are hands-on exhibits and information on nuclear energy.

The regional impact of Supply System operations is not limited to its role as a large-scale generator of electricity. It also has a considerable impact on state tax revenues. The Supply System pays several million dollars annually in generation taxes. This tax, based on 1.5 percent of the wholesale value of the electricity generated, is distributed to schools throughout Washington, as well as to local taxing districts. The state also receives sales and use taxes on nuclear fuel, materials, and services purchased by the Supply System. In addition, the Supply System's annual payroll is more than $66 million for its 1,500 employees.

Public utilities will face new challenges in the future. Supply System initiatives in continuing its program of reliable generation at operating plants, maintaining its industry-known employee training programs, continuing efforts to preserve Projects 1 and 3 for future completion, and examining alternatives to extend the life of the HGP are evidence of the organization's commitment to the future.

▲ ▲ ▲
Systems are constantly inspected and monitored to ensure the safe operation of Plant 2.

KONA AM/FM Tri-Cities Communications

▲ ▲ ▲

Tri-Cities Communications' KONA AM/FM radio station is located in Pasco, just across the blue bridge.

▲ ▲ ▲

One of KONA's disc jockeys broadcasts from the station's main control room.

Tri-Cities Communications' story began in February 1948, when a small AM radio station with the call letters KWIE went on the air in Kennewick. In 1953 the station was purchased by a television station, and together they became KEPR Television and Radio. After a fire gutted the station in 1963, it moved to Pasco, just across the blue bridge on Lewis Street. Then, in 1969, the television station was sold, and KEPR Radio was required to change its call letters.

Dean Mitchell, the manager, had heard about a station in Hawaii that was about to go off the air. It wanted a name that was easy to remember and took the Hawaiian station's call letters KONA. At about the same time KONA added FM band 105.3. In 1974 KONA moved to its current location at 2823 West Lewis in Pasco. By 1978 Dean Mitchell began purchasing the station and became owner and general manager. Staffing at the station grew from a couple of disc jockeys in the late 1940s to its current staff of 18 people.

KONA has become known as the Tri-Cities information station for news, sports, and weather, with 5,000 watts of power on AM 610 and 100,000 watts of power on FM 105.3. The station broadcasts to 33 counties in Washington, Oregon, and Idaho, 24 hours per day. KONA is committed to keeping the community informed about local and regional issues. After more than 40 years on the air, KONA is now the only station that is locally owned and operated.

The station attributes its success to an adult-contemporary format that appeals to local audiences and emphasizes news coverage. More than 20 percent of air time is devoted to news, and the majority of that news is local. News block times are featured at 7 a.m., noon, and 5 p.m. KONA uses ABC and CBS networks for top national and international news. Paul Harvey is featured three times daily. KONA is also the sports information station, broadcasting all the Tri-City high school basketball and football games on both AM and FM, as well as all the University of Washington Huskies games and the Seattle Seahawks games.

KONA's staff members are also active in both civic and professional organizations. Mitchell has served on the boards of the Tri-City Visitor and Convention Bureau, the Tri-City Industrial Development Council (TRIDEC), the Kennewick Housing Authority, and First Federal Savings Bank. Dean was also named Tri-Citian of the Year in 1982. The station is a member of the National Association of Broadcasters, the Washington State Association of Broadcasters, and the Radio Advertising Bureau. KONA has received many awards from the Associated Press for local news and sports reporting.

The station's management team is made up of radio veterans and includes Loyd Aman, production director who has been with the company for more than 25 years, and Dick Carstens, sales manager who has more than 20 years with KONA. Mitchell believes there will always be a place for a local station such as KONA. He plans to continue KONA AM/FM Tri-Cities Communication's popular format as long as it responds to the needs of the community.

Perseus Gourmet Products

Perseus vinegars are vinegar artistry. They are the fresh young greens of Gourmet, the spicy flavors of Sabroso, the sweet and mellow pinks of Sageberry, the full-bodied sweetness of Vinagré Bluet, the fruity and rich taste of Raspberry, and the enlivened flavors of Peach-Ginger. Each bottling of Perseus is carefully formulated by hand to assure its unique character and beauty. Organically grown in the Columbia Basin, Perseus ingredients are all natural. Perseus Gourmet Products is one of

▲▲▲
With the ingredients organically grown in the Columbia Basin, Perseus vinegars are formulated by hand and are of the highest quality.

the Tri-Cities homegrown success stories.

The story begins with two sisters: Kay Hansen and Penny Morgan, who because of a growing concern over the health of their father, decided to do something about it. One evening in 1984, Hansen learned that vinegar would help monitor his blood-sugar levels, cleanse his body, and relieve some of his pain of arthritis. Hansen and Morgan started a business to produce vinegar, and Perseus Gourmet Products was born.

Vinegars brewed in the kitchen achieved overnight success, and the

sisters found that they needed a larger facility. Perseus moved into an incubator at the Port of Kennewick's Oak Street industrial site, and with the expanded production capability, the business took off. Today Perseus products are sold across the state, on the East and West coasts, and in Canada, Australia, Japan, Malaysia, and, most recently, in Europe.

Perseus uses the best chardonnay and rice wines available in the Northwest. The wine is fermented for eight months to ensure the highest quality vinegars. The vinegars are poured into the finest wine bottles, and herbs such as basil, Italian parsley, tarragon, and garlic, as well as red pepper, shallots, and other culinary ingredients picked daily are added by hand.

All the herbs used in Perseus products are grown locally on land managed by the sisters. Herbs are harvested until Halloween, when they go into production of the fruit line. The herbs are also sold to produce houses for use in restaurants statewide. In addition to homegrown herbs, a visit to the farms is a feast for the senses. Hundreds of marigolds guard the precious herbs against insects, along with a colorful array of Morgan and Hansen's favorite flowers. Perseus recently expanded its product line to supply flowers to area florists. Morgan and Hansen's motto is, "Plant what makes the heart feel good."

Two sisters, one a homemaker and one a paralegal, joined forces and created a dynamic team. They had a great idea and were persistent. Hansen expanded the product line

and tested each new vinegar, while Morgan researched the marketplace and systematically expanded her marketing efforts to include national and international buyers. She used a three-pronged approach to marketing Perseus vinegars: as a fine-food item, as a gift item, and as a health food.

Morgan has also become a spokesperson for small business and was appointed to the Governor's Small Business Advisory Council. Perseus Gourmet Products is a member of the National Association for the Specialty Food Trade and Western United States Agricultural Trade Association, and participates in trade shows at the national and international levels.

Perseus promises products for the palates of those who prefer vinegar artistry to vinegar adequacy. At Perseus Gourmet Products, the company's reputation is built on using only the finest ingredients to create a product of nature's art.

▲▲▲
Each bottle of Perseus vinegar has a unique character, containing the finest herbs and wines.

BCS Richland, Inc. (BCSR)

In 1971 The Boeing Company, Seattle, established Boeing Computer Services (BCS) in order to consolidate its computing operations and provide information services to external markets. The division began with about $250 million of computing equipment and a staff of 2,700 employees who previously supported Boeing operations. Products and services included providing processing time on Boeing's own computer network to external users, developing specialized computer programs, systems integration, training, and consulting.

In 1975 BCS won the contract to provide computing services to the Energy Research and Development Administration (ERDA), the Department of Energy's (DOE) predecessor, and its contractors at

▲ ▲ ▲
A fish-eye view of the Network Control Center.

▲ ▲ ▲
Senior illustrator John Lawson demonstrates graphic illustration capabilities to BCSR president Ben Dole.

Hanford. BCS Richland, Inc. (BCSR), was formed as a subsidiary of The Boeing Company. The computer center that BCSR was selected to manage was one of the largest scientific data centers in the northwestern United States at that time. Located in the Federal Building in Richland, the CDC CYBER 74 computer was extended to Hanford user locations by a network reaching approximately 100 user terminals. Approximately 240 data-processing professionals made up the BCSR team in Richland. The five-year $60-million contract was the biggest commercial contract in BCS history. BCSR was awarded

▲ ▲ ▲
Hanford's Super Computer CRAY X-MP/18.

contract extensions in 1980 and 1985. The Boeing success at Hanford has provided experience and reputation for competitive wins of contracts with other government agencies.

In 1987 the Westinghouse Hanford Company, with BCSR as a subcontractor, assumed the DOE Operations and Engineering contract at Hanford. This contract consolidated activities previously performed by BCSR, Rockwell, Kaiser, Battelle, and Westinghouse. BCSR expanded staffing from 480 people just before consolidation to more than 1,000 at consolidation. The company functions as the Information Resource Management Department of Westinghouse and provides information services for the Hanford site. The information services include computing, telecommunications, and additional information services that can

benefit from automation.

Computing and telecommunications services currently include the operation of large-scale computer systems including a CRAY Super Computer, a sitewide data network connecting approximately 5,000 microcomputers and the mainframes, specialized minicomputers, a computer store for microcomputers and software, telephone service management, computer training, scientific and administrative software development, and technical consulting.

Through its library of programs, BCSR provides computer assistance in such areas as general business, nuclear-reactor technology, chemical processes, physics and applied mathematics, ecology, metallurgy, biology, and health physics. Computing staff members design data systems for a variety of purposes, including development of computer models for solving problems ranging from structural analysis and environmental studies to inventory control.

Additional information services include site mail, records manage-

ment and document control, word processing, photography, audiovisual production, graphic services, technical writing and editing, forms control, duplication, and printing. Automation of these additional services has proceeded with implementation of a 4,000-user electronic mail system, growth and diversification of desktop publishing, introduction of electronic forms, and plans to move Hanford's operations in the direction of a paperless office of the future.

Plans are in place to continue the technical support for Hanford programs with the acquisition of an advanced telephone system that will support both voice and data transmission with high-speed fiber-optic technology, higher capacity computer systems, and increased use of automated systems throughout Hanford operations.

Boeing also recognizes the importance of community support. In 1988 the firm committed $400,000 over three years to the Tri-City Industrial Development Council's diversification program to reduce the community's dependence on government funding sources. The company and individual employees also support a variety of community activities and service organizations.

BCSR's priorities are to do a quality job, on time and within budget. Employees are justifiably proud of their accomplishments since 1975 and are committed to continually improving the quality of their products and services.

In 1990 BCS Richland, Inc., celebrates 15 years in the Tri-Cities and hopes to make total quality the key to remaining a corporate citizen for at least another 15 years.

▲ ▲ ▲
Media specialist Dan Berg edits videotape production using the computer-controlled Edit Bay 1.

Sandvik Special Metals Corporation

▲ ▲ ▲
ABOVE: SSM employees prepare to load zirconium tubing into a cold pilgering machine.

LEFT: A lab technician checks tubes to ensure that no internal flaws exist.

Sandvik Special Metals Corporation (SSM), acknowledged as a leading supplier of zirconium and titanium alloy tubing for the nuclear and aerospace industries, continually sets quality and performance standards worldwide. At SSM's 130,000-square-foot production facility in Finley, nearly 400 highly trained and skilled individuals work with state-of-the-art equipment and innovative techniques to deliver tubing of un-equaled quality.

SSM was founded in 1966 as a result of the Atomic Energy Commission's diversification program for the Hanford Atomic Works in Richland. SSM's original nuclear divi-

sion began producing zirconium tubing in January 1968 using a newly developed and patented cold reduction process invented at SSM's parent company, Sandvik AB of Sweden. SSM has continued to refine and advance this process to produce its high quality products.

SSM is one of the world's largest

▲ ▲ ▲
Mark Calcavecchia swings a Ti-Shaft™ golf shaft.

manufacturers of zircaloy cladding for the nuclear industry. With years of experience in the research and development of zirconium tubing, SSM is qualified to produce titanium tubing of the highest quality with unique mechanical properties and

close tolerances. By combining space-age metals, sophisticated metallurgical technology, and expert design with meticulous care in processing, SSM produces optimum performance special metals.

In the 1980s, responding to the growing demand for other high-technology metals, SSM expanded the nuclear division to include aerospace industry applications. Titanium hydraulic tubing is produced by SSM for Airbus and Saab, along with European and U.S. military aircraft and helicopters. Titanium tubing has also been developed for medical applications. Titanium tubes can be safely implanted into human bones in cases of severe fractures.

In 1985 a separate sports division was created, and SSM began production of titanium tubing for sports applications. SSM purchased the patent for titanium shafts and developed the Ti-Shaft™, a titanium golf shaft that is commercially produced. Ti-Shafts™ were developed because of titanium's

▲ ▲ ▲
Sandvik's administration building is connected to the manufacturing plant by a sky bridge.

exceptional strength-to-weight ratio. The advantages of the shaft are its lightweight, torque resistance, durability, improved accuracy, and marked gains in driving distance. Ti-Shafts™ are available in golf pro shops worldwide.

In 1989 SSM's Titanium Sports Division began producing titanium component parts for mountain bikes such as handlebars, front forks, frames, seat tubes, and stems. Also under development are titanium pool cues and sports rackets for tennis and racquetball.

As part of a continuing commitment to the Tri-Cities, SSM has been the title sponsor for the annual Sandvik Washington Open Golf Tournament, a major Northwest Professional Golfers' Association event. Proceeds from the tournament are donated to the Blue Mountain Council of the Boy Scouts of America.

SSM is a wholly-owned subsidiary of Sandvik AB, which is one of Sweden's largest exporters, with 160 subsidiary companies in 50 countries. Sandvik consists of Sandvik AB, the parent company, plus six separate business areas, four regional companies, and two service companies.

Neil F. Lampson Inc.

Throughout the world, on construction and heavy-rigging projects, Neil F. Lampson Inc. cranes are synonymous with the best in the business. The name reflects a certain genius and creative energy represented in Neil F. Lampson himself.

The company builds, operates, maintains, sells, rents, and provides consulting services for the largest fleet of conventional and unconventional cranes in the world. It is a multimillion-dollar business that began with a Model-T Ford that was purchased by Neil in 1932 to haul fruits and vegetables from local farms to storage warehouses for shipping. Neil has spent many years establishing a company that carries the theme, "Progress Through Innovation."

Neil F. Lampson Inc. is recognized in the industry for three major innovations. The first came in the 1960s, when Lampson designed and constructed the first crawler transporter, which functions as a foundation for the Lampson cranes. The Lampson crawler is state of the art and can transport up to 4,000 tons on a single unit.

The second innovation came in the 1970s, when Lampson designed and constructed the Lampson Transi-Lift™, the largest capacity mobile crane in the world. The lift capacity of the first Lampson Transi-Lift™ was 300 tons and today ranges from 400 to 2,000 tons. The third innovation came in the 1980s, when Neil designed and constructed the Lampson Dynamic Compactor (LDC) or "thumper," which provides a cost-effective alternative to conventional methods of compaction. The LDC is designed specifically to reduce equipment wear and increase safety and ease of operation.

Neil F. Lampson Inc. owns and operates more than 250 major units of heavy-lift equipment, truck cranes, conventional crawler cranes with optional attachments, Lampson-manufactured Transi-Lift™ cranes, and crawler transporters. Lampson's fleet of heavy-rigging equipment is by far the most modern and versatile in the

▲ ▲ ▲

ABOVE: Neil F. Lampson, chief executive officer. Courtesy, Precision Photo Services

LEFT: William Lampson, president. Courtesy, Precision Photo Services

world today.

Since Lampson crawlers and cranes support projects worldwide, Neil believed that it was necessary to establish satellite sales offices to better serve customers' needs and to expand existing markets. With sales offices strategically located in Chicago, Denver, Honolulu, Houston, Portland, San Francisco, Los Angeles, Phoenix, and Seattle, as well as international offices in Sydney, Australia, and Calgary, Alberta, Canada, Lampson has gained a dominant market position in the crawler-transporter and crane-rental industry.

Neil F. Lampson Inc. is the parent company for other Lampson divisions: Columbia Pacific Transport Company, heavy-haul trucking division; Ranney Method Western Corporation, design and installation of municipal and industrial water

▲ ▲ ▲
Lampson's first diesel truck and semitrailer, 1938.

systems; Riggers Manufacturing Company, manufacturer of heavy-lift and transport equipment; and Lampson Universal Rigging, Inc., contracting and engineering division.

The corporation began in the Tri-Cities and will remain there, even though Neil has had ample opportunities to relocate. His glass-encased building, located in Kennewick at the base of the Cable Bridge, overlooks the Columbia River. Lampson's roots are deeply embedded in the Tri-Cities. "The communities of Kennewick, Pasco, and Richland have been good to us," he says. "We have the best of all worlds here. For our needs, there is perfect rail service, fine highways, and a good labor force with intelligent craftsmen who are second to none. There's also plenty of room around here—enough to do anything if you're man enough to try."

The founder's unencumbered thinking and belief that anything is possible has assured his company's continued success. Neil's attitude has been an important driver in the business and has been communicated to his son, Bill, who took over the day-to-day management of the firm in 1982.

Neil credits his son for much of the organization's growth in recent years. Bill has tripled the company's size since he took on the job. He

rarely disagrees with his father on how the business should be run. "We're too much alike. I run the business on a day-to-day basis, but his guidance is always present." Bill says his father raised him "more by example than discipline. But when you step out of bounds, you know it." Neil has shaped the man Bill is, as Neil was also shaped by his own father.

Neil's father was in the fruit and produce business as well as operating a farm in east Kennewick, where

▲ ▲ ▲
ABOVE: Neil F. Lampson Inc. corporate headquarters in Kennewick.

BELOW: One of the firm's projects was Tri-Cities Coliseum. This photo shows placement of the main trusses over the coliseum using Lampson cranes.

▲ ▲ ▲
The Lampson fleet in the early 1960s.

Neil still resides with his wife, Billie. Neil's father loved being in business and was always working on a new project, which generally involved Neil and his brother, Spike. Neil learned early that "with hard work and fair play there was compensation." At age 14, Neil sewed potato sacks for 14 cents per hour. When most of his friends were playing football, baseball, and basketball, "I did my chores. But believe me, it was a long way from drudgery." Even though his favorite pastimes included hunting, fishing, dances, swimming, and dating, Neil concedes that "my work was the most fun of all."

After Neil became an entrepreneur in 1932 with his one-ton Model-T Ford hauling fruits and vegetables, he bought larger trucks and eventually a semitrailer that he used to haul bigger loads over longer distances. Everything went reasonably well until the fall of 1935, when his father died from a ruptured lung. "If I am successful, I can thank my wonderful father for those early lessons and for giving me the opportunity to do something on my own. I believe that it is important to give those around you a chance to think and do for themselves—especially your own family," he says.

Neil helped his mother on the farm, and "by the grace of God and a little help from Mom," managed to graduate with his class in 1936. In addition to helping his mother and continuing with the hauling, Neil learned to fly in 1939. The following year he married Billie Jane Markham. When World War II started, Neil sold the trucks and became a flight instructor, eventually joining the Air Corps. He was assigned to the 556th Ferry Group, U.S. Army Transport Command, and learned to fly the P-40, P-47, P-39, P-63, and P-51, as well as all of the other U.S. Army aircraft.

Throughout the many years Neil flew, he had several incidents with engine and electrical failures, but he

▲ ▲ ▲
A portion of today's Lampson truck fleet.

learned to "remain calm, think it out, and go to work on the best possible solutions." When the war was over, he took his $6,200 in Army pay and lost it all in a craps game. "The lesson I learned from the experience was 'Don't gamble beyond what you can afford to lose,'" he says.

With the help of his wife, Billie, Neil purchased two trucks and a truck crane after the war. Billie managed an office in the garage, and Neil continued to buy and sell equipment or lease heavy equipment. He got a few good contracts and a few bad ones, but in 1954 he got his first real break: the rigging contract for the construction of the Phillips Chemical Company (now Chevron Chemical Company) ammonia plant.

By 1956 Lampson had incorporated. During the next 10 years the company did a variety of oil and power-related jobs in the Northwest and Alaska. In 1967 the firm contracted the heavy rigging for Colyear Chemical at Keni, Alaska. On this job, Lampson designed a portable, self-powered crawler transporter, using conventional side frames and pads from two crawler cranes; built a car body and bolster between the frames; and built a diesel-driven power package to drive the tracks. While the first crawler was somewhat primitive, it did the job efficiently and immediately received worldwide publicity.

Soon Neil F. Lampson Inc. was developing crawler transporters for service in Aruba, France, England, Scotland, Italy, Russia, Libya, Curaçao, Venezuela, and the Far

▲ ▲ ▲
Neil F. Lampson Inc.'s two largest cranes at the Port of Pasco are the largest mobile cranes in the world. In the foreground is a 1,200-ton-capacity crane, and in the background is a 2,000-ton-capacity crane.

East. The firm also secured several other rigging jobs that required heavy-lifting techniques, equipment, and personnel. At the same time Lampson was working on rigging jobs within the continental U.S. and Canada for oil and nuclear-power companies.

In about 1971 Lampson designed the Transi-Lift™. It took five years to secure the U.S. patents for the system. In 1978 he bid on a heavy-rigging job for a nuclear plant that required a 600-ton lift. Lampson developed the crane at a cost of several million dollars and tested it in the spring of 1979 with a 1,100-ton test weight and 280 feet of boom at a 100-foot radius—a feat that was unheard of anywhere in the industry for a fully mobile crawler crane. The savings to the power companies by using the Transi-Lift™ was several million dollars.

Lampson secured more rigging

▲ ▲ ▲

A Phillips Petroleum plant construction project. Lampson's entire fleet worked on this job, the first major project and the beginning of Lampson's successful company.

jobs, particularly in other countries. The largest machine the firm ever built was designed and sold to Hitachi in Japan for the construction of five nuclear-power plants. The Lampson Transi-Lift™ system continues to operate on projects in Japan, Korea, England, Scotland, Canada, and Norway. The U.S. flag flies on equipment on every Lampson project, along with the flag of the country in which it is operating.

For Neil Lampson, the business is very important. He credits his success to a willingness to give all his employees the opportunity to prove themselves on their own. Crane operators apprentice for up to five years, then start with small cranes and work up to larger cranes. There are more than 50 family-related employees working together at Lampson. Very few employers can boast that kind of loyalty. Lampson encourages that loyalty by showing an active interest in all phases of company operations. He walks the facility daily, greeting his employees by their first names and showing a keen interest in their activities. Lampson's heart and soul is present in every aspect of the organization.

His presence is also felt throughout the community. For 10 years Lampson has sponsored the annual 5K and 10K Cable Bridge Run. He also supports Little League. Since 1965 Lampson has donated cranes to lift the hydroplanes out of dry dock and into the Columbia River for the annual Columbia Cup races.

Among his peers in the Specialized Carriers and Rigging Association, an international organization of more than 700 members, Lampson has been honored with the Heavy-Rigging Job of the Year Award on three separate occasions. This award is presented annually to the heavy-rigging contractor who has engineered and completed the most unusual or difficult major rigging job using innovative rigging techniques or equipment. Lampson has also been awarded the Outstanding Safety Award by the association.

Neil Lampson is considered by many to be the Tri-Cities' international ambassador. According to former Kennewick city manager Joe Painter, there is "no bigger cheerleader for our area, and he carries our message to a whole lot of places. He takes a low profile. But when Neil speaks, people listen."

Neil prefers not to take all the credit for the success of the company. "Nobody ever did anything by themselves. It takes people, a lot of hardworking, good people, to make anything go. The rest of it is a willingness to be a doer and a lot of luck." Whatever the reason, Neil F. Lampson Inc. continues to be one of the most dynamic forces in the industry today.

Westinghouse Electric Corporation

On October 31, 1865, a 19-year-old George Westinghouse received his first patent and launched a career of invention and leadership that spanned a half-century of industrial progress. The company he founded continues to develop technology for the future.

Westinghouse technology played a key role in the development of the Pacific Northwest and the mid-Columbia region. The nation's first practical system for transmitting electricity over long distances happened a century ago in the 14 miles between Willamette Falls and Portland, using equipment designed and built by Westinghouse. And one of the nation's first successful long-distance transmission systems using alternating current—a Westinghouse system—ran 153 miles from Snoqualmie Falls to Seattle, Tacoma, and Everett in 1897. It is still in operation today, little changed from the original concept and copied worldwide.

During America's race to develop nuclear weapons ahead of its foes in

▲▲▲

The Fast Flux Test Facility at Hanford, designed, built, and operated by Westinghouse, is the most versatile test reactor in the world for advanced nuclear research programs. The white dome is the reactor containment building, in which the reactor vessel and all major operating components are located. The surrounding dark towers are heat exchangers, part of the reactor coolant system.

World War II, Westinghouse was one of six leading equipment suppliers for the Manhattan Project. The project first took shape on the 560-square-mile Hanford Site in 1943 and helped transform small riverfront farm communities into today's diversified Tri-Cities.

Westinghouse Electric Corporation officially came to the Hanford Site in 1970 to operate the Hanford Engineering Development Laboratory and build the Fast Flux Test Facility (FFTF), a unique test facility for liquid-metal fast-breeder reactors. The project was not new to Westinghouse, which had joined the breeder reactor program in 1968 as a subcontractor to Battelle Northwest for FFTF core design.

The FFTF has been in operation since 1982 and, as the most versatile test reactor in the world, is the cornerstone of advanced nuclear research programs. The FFTF is capable of carrying out many important development projects, such as the production of several medical and commercial isotopes, including gadolinium-153, used in the diagnosis of osteoporosis, a crippling bone disease.

The FFTF has also been used by scientists in the United States, Great Britain, Japan, West Germany, France, Switzerland, and Canada to develop improved safety features for advanced reactors and to test materials for fusion reactor development and space reactor technology.

In 1983 the Department of Energy (DOE), the Department of Defense, and NASA initiated a three-phase space development program.

Its plans include a new space reactor system to meet the large electric power requirements of civilian and military space missions in the future. A prototype system is to be tested by Westinghouse Hanford Company in a simulated space environment at the Hanford Site.

In 1987 Westinghouse Hanford Company became DOE's sole operations and engineering contractor for the site. At the forefront of Westinghouse's mission at Hanford is the environmental restoration of the site. In 1989 a landmark agreement was reached between DOE, the Washington State Department of Ecology, and the U.S. Environmental Protection Agency to clean up nearly 50 years of nuclear wastes generated by Hanford activities The agreement will ensure that activities are conducted in an environmentally sound manner for the safety of Hanford workers and their neighbors in the Pacific Northwest. The cleanup, expected to take 30 years, uses innovative waste-disposal techniques. Methods for permanent disposal of liquid wastes include their conversion into solid materials.

Westinghouse also has lead responsibility for the Hanford Site's decontamination and decommissioning program. The program comprises the expertise needed to carry out major decontamination and decommissioning projects on a variety of facilities, including eight retired nuclear reactors at Hanford.

Westinghouse also continues to perform Hanford's original defense production mission, processing the last of the uranium fuel that was converted to plutonium in Hanford's N Reactor for use in defense programs. Operation of the N Reactor ceased in 1987 because of a decline in the need for plutonium. Westinghouse will continue to maintain the reactor in case it is needed again.

When Westinghouse Hanford Company was awarded the Hanford

operations and engineering contract in 1987, its parent company, Westinghouse Electric Corporation, made significant commitments to help diversify and develop the economic base of the Tri-City area. One was the establishment of the Westinghouse Tri-Cities Investment Management Company. Another was the establishment of the Westinghouse Northwest Environmental Center.

The Westinghouse Tri-Cities Investment Management Company was a unique entity in the community, providing venture-capital funds to help new or expanding technology-oriented businesses in the area. In addition to providing seed money, the organization brought the community a channel to Westinghouse Electric Corporation's diverse business resources and expertise.

The Investment Management Company also recognized the importance of education to the community. The firm pledged up to $100,000 annually (over a five-year period) to local educational development programs. In addition to cash contributions, the company searched the parent corporation for opportunities to bring its professional resources and expertise to Tri-Cities schools and educational programs.

The Investment Management Company sponsored formation of the first Tri-Cities Entrepreneurs Club. The club meets monthly and fosters a community network of entrepreneurs who share experiences, accomplishments, and challenges.

The Investment Management

▲ ▲ ▲

Many power stations throughout the Northwest produce electricity with generators designed by Westinghouse—including the mighty Grand Coulee, which boasts the world's largest generators. Hydropower fueled many of the early applications of George Westinghouse's alternating current concept.

Company completed its mission of investing $5 million in venture capital to assist new Tri-City businesses in April 1990. At that time it turned more than $185,000 worth of stock holdings and financial support to the newly formed venture-capital firm, Benton-Franklin Ventures, Inc. Included in that transfer were $150,000 worth of stock in two young Kennewick enterprises and $35,000 to assist in the startup of Benton-Franklin Ventures, which will continue the venture development efforts started by the Westinghouse Investment Management Company.

The Westinghouse Northwest Environmental Center in Richland offers a wide range of environmental engineering, laboratory analysis, asbestos assessment, and hazardous waste management and consultation services.

The center's staff advises regional and national clients of applicable environmental regulations and assists in preparation of facility reports and remedial programs. They provide assessment of underground storage tank integrity to ensure compliance with

requirements for leak detection, corrosion protection, spill/overfill prevention, and treatment of groundwater using the Modular Product Recovery and Groundwater Treatment System, a mobile unit that can be quickly dispatched to a site where tank leakage or spills threaten groundwater.

The center added a solid material characterization laboratory to its Richland facility in 1988 to analyze materials that may contain asbestos or other fiber substances. The laboratory uses state-of-the-art instrumentation, including a transmission-electron microscope, scanning-electron microscope, X-ray diffraction system, and high-quality optical microscopes. Analyses are routinely performed for school districts, apartment complexes, hospitals, department stores, and other public facilities.

In 1989 the staff and services offered by the Westinghouse Northwest Environmental Center expanded considerably, and a second office, housing environmental engineering, was opened in Kennewick.

▲ ▲ ▲

Scientists at the Westinghouse Northwest Environmental Center in Richland use specialized state-of-the-art equipment such as this scanning transmission electron microscope to detect asbestos fibers in air samples—just one of the many environmental management services provided at the center.

United Express/ NPA, Inc.

The United Express story began in 1986 when a group of airline professionals joined together to form NPA, Inc., based in the Tri-Cities. According to Craig Belmondo, president of the company, the Tri-Cities fit into the plan by providing demographic advantages, a strong business base, necessary operational and maintenance facilities, easy access to marketing partner United Airlines' gateway cities, and an unparalleled desire on the part of the local community to make the enterprise work.

United Express inaugurated air service with 12 nonstop flights between Pasco and Seattle on July 27, 1987. Within two weeks more nonstop service had been added between Pasco and Portland. By the end of the year service had been expanded to seven Northwest cities. By the conclusion of 1989 United Express offered more than 250 daily flights to 15 cities in four states, utilizing a fleet of 25 aircraft, including the 30-passenger Embraer Brasilia

▲ ▲ ▲
Craig Belmondo, president of United Express/NPA, Inc.

▲ ▲ ▲
United Express' Embraer Brasilia, a 30-passenger aircraft.

and the 19-passenger British Aerospace Jetstream 31. The firm has developed hubs at all major United Airlines gateway cities throughout the Pacific Northwest.

United Express employs more than 600 people, with more than half of them located in the Tri-Cities. Belmondo plans to increase staff during the next three years to accommodate the airlines' growth in existing markets, as well as new markets in the Pacific Northwest.

Currently the business traveler accounts for 80 percent of the airlines' revenue, with the remaining provided by vacation travelers. Belmondo plans to modify those percentages to a 70/30 split by accessing the leisure market with the creation of group, charter, and weekend packages. United Express passengers enjoy coordinated schedules with United for a minimum layover time, same-terminal connections, advance check in and seat assignments, automatic baggage transfers, and a minimum of 500 Mileage Plus miles on every United Express flight.

United Express also provides reliable and quick small package and cargo service throughout the Pacific Northwest. This allows for door-to-door same-day and overnight deliveries. In addition, the United Express partnership with United Airlines provides counter-to-counter

shipments to more than 200 cities in the continental United States, Hawaii, and Alaska.

United Express is headquartered at the Tri-Cities Regional Airport in Pasco. It is a wholly owned subsidiary of California-based WestAir Holding, Inc., named 1988 Commuter/ Regional Airline of the Year by *Air Transport World,* the industry's leading professional journal. WestAir Holding, Inc., is the largest regional airline system in the nation.

Belmondo attributes United Express' success to investing in the company's staff by providing training, resources, and a corporate environment that will allow employees to perform in a safe and professional manner; developing service in smaller markets free of substantial competition from larger jet carriers; continuing to enhance the partnership with United Airlines by steadily increasing customers that connect with United flights; and maintaining fleet flexibility by matching the machine to the mission. United Express will continue to meet those objectives as it evaluates new opportunities for growth and diversification.

Our Lady of Lourdes Health Center

Our Lady of Lourdes Health Center is the oldest "new" hospital in the Tri-Cities. The health center began in 1916, when the Sisters of St. Joseph of Carondelet were called to Pasco to sponsor a health care ministry. By 1921 a new 55-bed hospital had been built. The following year the Sisters founded a nursing school, and in 1925 the first nursing class graduated.

As the community grew, so did the need for expanded health care, and by 1950 construction began to add 35 more beds. The following year the hospital auxiliary was founded. Hospital services continued to be added, and in 1969 a four-room surgery and recovery facility was constructed. A new patient-care

▲ ▲ ▲

The Birthplace at Lourdes features a sensory-enriched nursery, assuring that every delivery is a positive family experience.

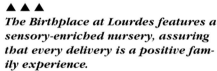

area was built in 1984 at a cost of $16.5 million.

In 1988 Our Lady of Lourdes Health Center and the 32-bed Carondelet Psychiatric Care Center in Richland became part of the Health Care Corporation of the Sisters of St. Joseph of Carondelet, which includes facilities in nine states.

Our Lady of Lourdes Health Center, in addition to providing traditional health care services, has also been a front-runner in creating programs that respond to the changing needs of the Tri-Cities' community. The hospital's original maternity ward is now called the Birth-

▲ ▲ ▲

Our Lady of Lourdes Health Center in Pasco.

place at Lourdes and features birthing rooms and a sensory-enriched nursery, assuring that every delivery is a positive family experience.

Other innovative programs include an alcohol/drug treatment program, a physical-therapy/sports-medicine program, a radiology/nuclear medicine program, a diabetes education program, and Columbia Home Health, a joint hospital program to care for seriously ill or injured patients at home.

The Sisters, administration, doctors, and staff at Our Lady of Lourdes Health Center are committed to providing what is described as person-centered care, and the facility promises care that is compassionate toward all people.

Battelle Northwest Laboratories

From currency to clothes and medicines to building materials, much of America's life-style in the year 2000 is taking shape today at Battelle Memorial Institute. Whether it is identifying ways to rejuvenate our lakes and streams, deciphering genetic codes, or understanding global climate change, Battelle scientists are transforming scientific breakthroughs into essential technologies for the twenty-first century.

For more than 60 years the products of Battelle's research have become integral components of American lives everywhere. Innovations such as the Universal Product Codes on groceries, copper-nickel sandwich, the technology responsible for photocopiers, and the hologram on credit cards are all evidence of Battelle's dedication to improving the quality of life.

Battelle's technical evolution is the legacy of Gordon Battelle, who, in 1929, established what was to become the world's largest independent research organization. Now serving more than 2,000 government and business clients worldwide, Battelle has become a leading organization dedicated to putting science and technology to work by combining technical talent, experience, and equipment. That initiative, plus the spirit, drive, and dedication of Battelle's employees, have created an internationally recognized organization serving industry and government by developing, commercializing, and managing technology.

In 1965 Battelle assumed responsibility for managing and operating the U.S. Department of Energy's

Hanford Laboratory, which was renamed the Pacific Northwest Laboratory. Today, through a unique contractual agreement with the U.S. Department of Energy, $280 million worth of private and federal government laboratories and office space provide a quality setting for extensive scientific investigation and technology transfer. Battelle is located on 280 acres in Richland near the federal Hanford Site. Other facilities include the Marine Sciences Laboratory next to Sequim Bay in western Washington and the Battelle Seattle

▲ ▲ ▲

ABOVE: More than $280 million in private and federal government resources provide Battelle extensive capabilities for scientific investigation and technology transfer in Washington State.

LEFT: Scientists must interpret and understand vast amounts of information when investigating the intricacies of bioengineering and superconductivity—just two of the initiatives in progress at Battelle.

Research Center near the University of Washington. Since opening in the mid-1960s Battelle researchers have reported more than 2,100 inventions, and more than 270 patents have been issued on their inventions.

The Pacific Northwest Laboratory has evolved into one of the Department of Energy's major, multiprogram laboratories dedicated to several specific fields of research: environment, human health, national security, and energy. In its efforts, Battelle employs more than 3,500 scientists, engineers, and specialists whose collective efforts help to foster regional economic growth and contribute to improved U.S. competitiveness.

However, simply acquiring and possessing new knowledge is only part of the innovation process. The technical application of new and creative ideas is essential. One of

▲ ▲ ▲
ABOVE: Battelle research is attempting to mimic nature's strong materials by growing specially developed ceramic crystals in the laboratory in hopes of creating incredibly strong, energy-efficient materials.

RIGHT: Manny, the computer-controlled robot created by Battelle for the U.S. Army, reproduces complex body movements, simulates breathing, and even sweats while testing special clothing designed to withstand hazardous environments.

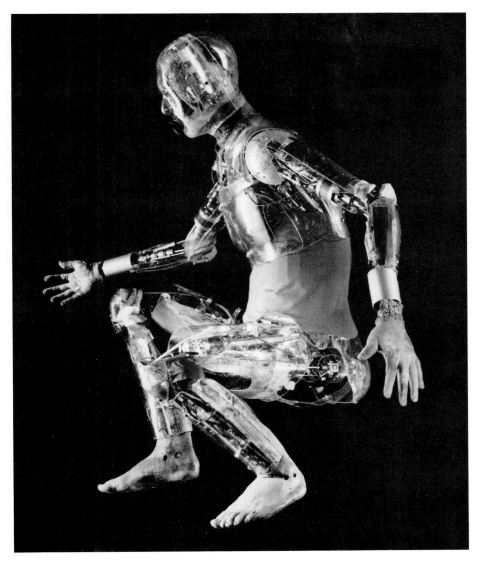

Battelle's most fulfilling missions is putting technology to work for the benefit and betterment of all mankind.

Battelle researchers, for example, have developed a technique for isolating hazardous chemical and radioactive wastes disposed of in the ground. Electric probes inserted in the soil cause both earth and waste to melt, transforming the materials, when cooled, into a material that resembles obsidian. This technique, with incredible possibilities for environmental cleanup, exemplifies how government-developed concepts and technologies can be transferred to private industry for commercial application.

Another technique developed by Battelle researchers converts ordinary sewage sludge into burnable oil, similar to diesel fuel. Full-scale plants are expected to provide large cities with a potential solution to sewage sludge disposal, while producing a clean, inexpensive source of energy.

Several U.S. companies are now marketing a product that prevents the growth of plant roots and unwanted vegetation for up to 100 years. Originally developed by Battelle to prevent roots from growing into low-level radioactive waste-disposal sites, the biobarrier is

currently eliminating weed problems on airport runways, sidewalks, tennis courts, and swimming pools.

A robotic mannequin, so lifelike it even breathes and sweats, was developed for the U.S. Army by Battelle engineering specialists to test protective clothing used in hazardous conditions. The robot, which also can test other types of clothing, such as thermal and athletic wear, offers promising applications for the private sector.

Biological research conducted at the firm's Marine Sciences Laboratory might help determine why some mussels and mollusks can overcome cancer-like abnormalities. Finding answers to these key questions could help find a treatment or cure for America's number-one killer—cancer.

Battelle scientists also are unraveling the secrets of nature to produce strong, flexible materials. This attempt to mimic biological processes may lead to incredible new building substances creating safer, more efficient construction materials.

Human activities have grown to a point that they now are resulting in environmental change on a global scale. Battelle researchers seek to better understand the dynamics of the earth's environment; how these actions may cause global warming, ozone depletion, and climate change; and, most important, how these issues can be addressed.

In the twenty-first century Battelle will continue to strive to provide the technical solutions to the world's most pressing problems. At its laboratories in the Tri-Cities, Battelle is developing critical new programs and facilities to support national science and technology needs.

The Molecular Science Research Center will provide the United States with its only center dedicated to molecular science research. It will bring biologists, chemists, physicists, materials, and computer scientists together to solve a wide range of problems in energy, environment, material and chemical sciences, health, and medicine.

The Environmental Sciences Research Center will formulate better strategies for environmental cleanup of hazardous chemicals and other substances that have seriously threatened the earth's fragile environment. The Environmental and Molecular Sciences Laboratory will support the molecular research needs of the two centers and serve as the focal point of molecular-level research in the United States.

Battelle's contributions are not limited to the scientific community. Being a leader in its own home community and a dedicated Northwest neighbor are equally important. Year after year Battelle and its employees support the theater, arts, education, cultural events, and quality of life activities that touch the entire community. Nearly $300,000 in employee and corporate contributions annually make their way to the United Way and its Washington State agencies for distribution to worthy organizations.

Generous contributions and grants are dedicated each year to worthy community programs and events. For instance, the Tri-Cities local public television and radio stations received

▲▲▲

LEFT: This sensitive new device, developed at Battelle, enables utilities and government agencies to better assess the potential of solar energy as well as allow researchers to monitor atmospheric pollutants and global climate change, and even design more energy-efficient buildings.

BELOW: Vitrification, a technique for incorporating nuclear waste into glass for long-term storage, has been under study at Battelle since the early 1960s. The technology is being used to support waste-disposal activities at Hanford.

Battelle support for initial development and continued program support. For more than a decade Battelle has supported the work of local artists through annual Art Purchase awards and contributions to the Northwest Young Artist Series.

Recognizing tomorrow's rewards for today's educational investment, Battelle supports a wide variety of educational science programs in the communities where it operates. For example, the company has committed thousands of dollars in annual college scholarships to graduates of Benton County and Franklin County high schools.

In addition, as operator of the Pacific Northwest Laboratory, Battelle manages advanced educational pro-

▲ ▲ ▲

RIGHT: Retired Battelle volunteers, working through the Tri-Cities Food Bank, help package food for hungry families in Richland. The United Way agency serves nearly 1,000 people per week.

BELOW: The molecular modeling laboratory at Battelle's Richland complex provides scientists involved in theoretical research with computer graphics hardware and software to enhance their research capabilities.

grams for the U.S. Department of Energy and adds its own resources, where appropriate, to extend assistance to schools and scholars at all levels of learning. Several hundred students and educators visit the laboratory each year to experience live science. In other programs, researchers visit schools to share their knowledge and excitement about science and technology. One such program has reached more than 15,000 students and teachers since it began in 1984.

At the university level, Battelle of-

fers a host of opportunities for faculty and students to participate in research programs at the laboratory. Formal collaborative agreements with the region's universities have provided a means for productive partnerships in education.

The next millennium with new uncertainties and challenging initiatives will test America's best minds. The nation will rely on science and technology to help it preserve and protect environmental quality and human health, explore and unravel the secrets of DNA, forecast and

respond to global climate change, enhance more efficient use of limited energy resources, and improve U.S. competitiveness in the global marketplace.

As Battelle Pacific Northwest Laboratories enters its next 25 years of service, it publicly renews its commitment to science in the service of all mankind. It is a time to stretch and strive for a more promising and prosperous future because, as Oliver Wendell Holmes once said, "The greatest thing in this world is not so much where we are, but in what direction we are moving."

Washington State University at Tri-Cities

▲▲▲
Many of WSU Tri-Cities' students are placebound professionals who wish to earn degrees without leaving the region. From left are Steve Desteese, electrical engineering student; Lynn Washington, chemical engineering student; and Quang Nguyen, Ph.D. candidate in electrical engineering. Photo by Charles Powell, WSU

Being an educational partner with the Tri-Cities is not a new relationship for Washington State University. WSU's first county extension agency was established in Benton County in 1913. During the late 1940s WSU's "people's university" provided continuing education courses in Pasco.

WSU began offering credit courses in 1946 as part of the General Electric School of Nuclear Engineering. In 1958 WSU became part of the multi-university Joint Center for Graduate Study at Hanford, and in 1985 it became part of the five-university consortium known as the Tri-Cities University Center, fiscally managed by the University of Washington.

In 1988 the state legislature designated WSU as the primary provider of upper-division and graduate-level education in the Tri-Cities. Culminating community and legislative efforts, WSU Tri-Cities officially was established in July 1989.

Under the direction of Dean James Cochran, WSU Tri-Cities offers six undergraduate programs and 14 master's programs ranging from liberal arts and sciences, education, and business to engineering and computer science. The branch campus

also provides continuing education classes, cooperative extension programs, consulting, research, cultural events, and public service.

Initial program expansion includes undergraduate nursing, and master's programs in education and environmental science. Several faculty positions as well as WSU's Small Business Development Center support the Tri-Cities diversification efforts and economic development. WSU Radio and TV Services continue public broadcasting efforts in the Tri-Cities.

Ground breaking for an addition

to triple the size of the center at 100 Sprout Road in Richland began in May 1990. The new facility will house classrooms, laboratories, a library, computing labs, telecommunications operations, and faculty offices. Enrollment, now at around 900 students, is expected to double or triple within the next two decades, depending on regional growth.

It is fitting that the Tri-Cities branch (along with Washington State University's two other branch campuses in Vancouver and Spokane) was launched on the 100th anniversary of the founding of WSU—a land-grant research university rich in the tradition of quality higher education.

▲▲▲
Several WSU Tri-Cities' classrooms overlook the Columbia River, as does this mechanical engineering class.

Kaiser Engineers Hanford

From roads in the Pacific Northwest to dams in South America, Henry J. Kaiser was a builder for more than 50 years. Today the tradition of engineering and building—and the vision of the future that he created—is carried forward by Kaiser Engineers Hanford (KEH).

The original company began in 1914 in Vancouver, Washington, as a paving and road construction firm. As the Kaiser companies grew and patriarch Henry became one of the nation's leading industrialists, that vision of the future kept the companies on the forefront of engineering and construction technologies.

Kaiser Engineers has led the way with some of America's most ambitious and well-known projects, such as Hoover Dam, Bonneville Dam, and Grand Coulee Dam. During World War II the seven West Coast shipyards that bore the Kaiser name turned out ships at an astonishing rate.

In the 1950s Kaiser Engineers came to the Tri-Cities to build the two Hanford K Reactors. Work at Hanford continued in the 1960s with construction of the N Reactor and the associated power generating plant. In 1982 Kaiser Engineers Hanford was named architect/ engineer for the Hanford Site. Since then, the company has conducted hundreds of projects at multiple locations at the site. In 1987 the firm was assigned construction responsibility as well.

Now KEH, a member of the American Capital and Research Corporation family of companies, is both architect/engineer and constructor for the Department of Energy (DOE) and its contractors engaged in chemical processing, nuclear waste management, reactor operations, environmental cleanup, and fuel fabrication.

Perhaps no other issue in the next decade will test the engineering and construction profession as much as the cleanup and management of hazardous and radioactive wastes. KEH offers an unequaled spectrum of engineering services to meet this challenge. Company services range from investigations that determine the extent of contamination at a site, to engineering feasibility studies of remedial actions, to the design and construction of systems to clean up, minimize, or destroy wastes.

In the defense waste arena, KEH engineers are busy designing systems that will be used for glassification of wastes so that they can be shipped and stored more safely. Construction forces, including

▲ ▲ ▲
An architectural model of a waste sampling characterization facility.

experts in asbestos abatement and decontamination, are performing work in compliance with federal and state environmental regulations.

Kaiser Engineers, a presence at Hanford for the past 40 years, is an integral part of the Tri-Cities community. KEH contributed $500,000 to higher education, including support of a master's program in engineering management at the Washington State University's Tri-Cities branch campus, the university's public television programming, and Columbia Basin College's building foundation. The firm takes an active leadership role in the annual Benton-Franklin United Way campaign as part of its community service program. Belief in the Tri-Cities as an ever-growing community led to KEH's major contribution to TRIDEC's Renaissance program.

The men and women of Kaiser Engineers Hanford are committed to the missions of the Hanford Site and are contributing citizens to the Tri-Cities community. These employees exemplify the credo so simply stated by the company's founder: "In working and growing, you can find ways of always keeping young, forever learning, always accepting new challenges and opportunities."

▲ ▲ ▲
Circa 1950s, 100K area under construction by Kaiser Engineers.

Chevron Chemical Company

It was more than 30 years ago that Art Mohr of California Spray Chemical Company announced plans for the construction of a new $4.5-million fertilizer plant in Kennewick to annually supply 80,000 tons of dry and liquid fertilizer to Northwest farmers. The new plant was constructed on 60 acres that bordered the Columbia River. During the open house in 1960 governors from nine western states attended the special event.

As agribusiness grew and developed in the Mid-Columbia region, so did the need for fertilizers precisely formulated for soils and crops in the area. In early 1968 the firm that became known as Chevron Chemical Company announced plans for a $3.5-million expansion program that would increase production capacity to 200,000 tons per year. The newly constructed plant produced nitric acid, ammonium nitrate, and Unipels™.

Chevron's Unipels™ are unique products that provide two forms of nitrogen and phosphorus in each BB-size pellet—one for quick bursts of plant growth and another for continued plant feedings. The product itself was packed in 80-pound bags. Ammonia, the raw material for fertilizer production, was supplied by a 1,500-foot pipeline from the nearby Phillips Pacific Chemical Plant.

As processes became more sophisticated, environmental laws became more stringent, competition became more intense, and farm technology was developed and refined, Chevron developed fertilizer solutions for direct application through irrigation systems. The first production expansion was soon sold out, which prompted a second expansion of $47.3 million in 1978 that increased production capacity from 200,000 tons to 550,000 tons annually. Major improvements included application of the latest technology

for environmental protection, an increased production capacity, added storage space, and installation of a streamlined shipping facility for bulk ammonium nitrate and complex fertilizer products.

The bulk storage and load-out system is considered the most advanced in the industry. The goal was to reach farmers in record time during the critical 60-day spring growing period. Chevron engineers designed load-out systems capable of moving fertilizer at a rate of 125 tons per hour. The new facilities were dedicated on August 21, 1978, by the president of Chevron Chemical. At that time it was the largest single capital-expenditure project in the firm's history.

Business boomed until 1981, when the U.S. government grain embargo, the rise of the dollar, crop controls, and competition, particularly from Canada in the fertilizer production business, caused a severe downturn. Since Chevron's business was tied directly to agriculture, it was not long before the firm was negatively impacted. The slump lasted for more than five years. Chevron's plant utilization dropped from 90 percent

▲▲▲
Two loadout towers speed direct bulk loading of trucks and railcars from warehouses that store up to 50,000 tons of NPK (Unipel) fertilizers. The facilities can ship up to 250 tons of product per hour.

to 60 percent.

The first step in the recovery process came in December 1986, when Chevron purchased the former Phillips Pacific Chemical Company ammonia plant. This allowed Chevron to manufacture ammonia for sale and provided a stable source of feedstock for fertilizer production.

Chevron was a survivor, and its commitment to the Tri-Cities and Columbia Basin would pay off in the late 1980s. Demand for Chevron products began to increase significantly due to changes in government programs that were favorable to farmers. More farm acres went into production, requiring Chevron plants to run at a much higher rate and capacity. The Chevron plant in Kennewick is the chemical company's largest fertilizer producer and sells 20 percent of the nitrogen fertilizer products used in Washington,

▲▲▲
A Chevron customer spreading dry fertilizer in the Pasco area.

Oregon, and Idaho. They also ship to California and Montana. Available irrigated land has significantly increased, resulting in more fertilizers tailored for irrigated farms.

Chevron is positive about the future of agriculture in the Tri-Cities and throughout the Northwest. As the cost to produce fruits and vegetables continues to increase in California, farmers will look to southeastern Washington to not only grow, but process their food products. The area has a ready supply of low-cost water and power, and plans are under way to develop Phase II of the Columbia Basin Project. The increased focus on agriculture in the area will ensure the long-term future of Chevron's facilities.

Chevron will also continue to set the standard in the industry for environmental compliance. The firm is committed to not only comply with the letter of the law, but the spirit of the law as well. Safety of plant employees is also a key commitment at Chevron, an organization that is recognized in the industry for safe plant operations. The company's ammonia plant was chosen from more than 300 fertilizer and agriculture chemi-

cal facilities nationwide, winning the National Safety Council's Merit Award for achievements in the area of safety in 1988. The plant also won the Chevron Chairman's Award for Safety that same year. Chevron's fertilizer plant has also been recognized for safe operations and has won the Chevron Chairman's Award for Safety in 1985, 1986, and 1987. Chevron employees contribute a wealth of experience and training to their jobs; most employees have been with Chevron at least 10 years.

Chevron Chemical Company is active in the farm community. It is a member of the Far West Fertilizer Association, Agribusiness Northwest, the Association of Washington Business, and the Fertilizer Institute. Locally Chevron is a member of TRIDEC, and many of the 170 employees are active members of the Kiwanis, Rotary Club, and other community organizations. Chevron's greatest community involvement is in

support of United Way.

Chevron has been recognized throughout the Columbia Basin as a major contributor to the growth and development of the Tri-Cities. It was the massive potential for agricultural expansion, resulting from the Columbia Basin Project, including the availability of raw materials, low utility rates, excellent transportation systems, a large available water supply, and a strong labor force, that attracted California Spray Chemical Company to the area more than 30 years ago.

The 1990s are expected to bring another boom in the agriculture business as more and more products are grown locally. Chevron Chemical Company will be there to provide the reliable product and services for which they have become known.

▲▲▲
The two Chevron facilities located near Finley. The ammonia plants are in the foreground, and the dry and liquid fertilizer plants are in the center of the picture. The two facilities are connected by pipeline. Courtesy, Precision Photo Services, Inc.

Benton County Public Utility District (PUD)

▲ ▲ ▲
ABOVE: The PUD's main office is located at Sixth and Auburn streets in Kennewick.

LEFT: Benton PUD is governed by three locally elected commissioners. Commissioners (left to right) Robert G. Graves, Francis J. Moore, and John A. Goldsbury celebrated 50 years of combined service to the PUD in July 1989.

Benton County PUD is a special purpose district of the State of Washington with the responsibility of providing electric service. The Public Utility District serves the urban areas of Kennewick, Prosser, and Benton City and most of the large irrigated farm developments in the county. Richland is served by its own city-owned electric system. The remainder of the county, which includes West Richland, is served by the

Benton Rural Electric Association. With approximately 110 employees and more than 1,200 miles of electric lines, the Benton County PUD is one of the larger consumer-owned utilities in the state.

The PUD is governed by three locally elected commissioners who serve six-year terms. The commission meets on a regular basis with meetings open to the public.

The PUD's formation was a result

of a grass-roots effort by citizens of the state, the Washington State Grange, and state labor organizations. In the early part of the century, electrical power was denied to many of the county's residents due to the high cost demanded by the privately owned power company serving the area to build the lines to deliver power to the countryside. The state legislature refused to enact legislation allowing the formation of public utility districts, so the matter was referred to the people of the state as a referendum in 1930.

The initiative passed. This—with the passage of the Bonneville Project Act and the Federal Rural Electrification Act, which resulted in the formation of rural electric cooperatives—paved the way for low-cost power to be delivered to all residents of

LEFT: A line crew performs maintenance using one of the PUD's modern bucket trucks.

BELOW: A state-of-the-art, computer-aided design and drafting system helps the PUD's engineering department perform line facility drawings. These drawings aid operations in line maintenance and construction.

more than 32,000 customers.

The PUD's electrical system is designed to handle the expanding needs of the community and is ready to serve new customers: commercial, industrial, residential, and agricultural. These customers enjoy power that costs less than four cents per kilowatt-hour. Currently, the national average is about eight cents per kilowatt-hour. The PUD will continue to enjoy a long-term power supply from the Bonneville Power Administration, from whom all its power is purchased.

Customer service is a high priority with the Benton County PUD. Many programs are provided as a free service, including conservation programs, school safety programs, and its community-wide public information program. The PUD also offers to its customers a level monthly payment program, low-interest loans for heat pumps, and discounts for low-income, disabled, and senior citizen customers.

As it enters the 1990s the Benton County Public Utility District continues its commitment to provide high-quality, dependable service. The utilization of computer technology in the PUD's operations assures an electric system with high reliability.

Benton County.

There was tremendous excitement as many homes and farms received electricity for the first time. Benton County farmers willingly helped crews string the wire. The PUD and the Benton Rural Electric Association held workshops to instruct residents in the use of electric appliances. Electricity helped ease many of the back-breaking chores farm families had to endure.

The Benton County PUD became an operating utility in 1946. It served 3,754 customers from its headquarters in Prosser. In 1955 the district moved into its current headquarters at Sixth and Auburn in Kennewick. Today the PUD provides electrical service to

City of Kennewick

The City of Kennewick is located in Benton County on the Columbia River, close to the point that the Yakima and Snake rivers join the Columbia. Kennewick and the nearby cities of Pasco and Richland comprise an area known as the Tri-Cities.

Kennewick's first residents were the Indian tribes who spent their winters fishing for salmon in the Yakima River and grazing their horses on the surrounding hills. The word "Kennewick" is presumed to be the Indian name for "Winter Heaven." The first recorded mention of the Tri-City area was made in

increased the population to 15,000 people by 1947. During the next 40 years Kennewick's continued population growth came as a result of immigration and annexation of Benton County lands. By the late 1980s the city's population grew to more than 37,000 people.

During the early years the railroad business and agriculture characterized Kennewick's major industries. The Columbia Basin Project with the following irrigation significantly expanded the agricultural products that could be grown in the area. More than 500,000 acres are committed to dryland farming, with an additional

▲▲▲
The public swimming pool in Kennewick.

▲▲▲
The Tri-Cities Coliseum was completed in 1988 and seats 6,000 people.

Lewis and Clark's journal when they camped at the confluence of the Snake and Columbia rivers on October 16, 1805.

The first white settler homesteaded there in 1883. Kennewick's incorporation in 1904 came as a result of the Northern Pacific Railroad's expansion to include the small township. A creamery was established in 1905 and a grape juice factory was established two years later. By 1940 the population of Kennewick had grown to more than 1,900 people. But the wartime activities at Hanford

160,000 acres for irrigated farming. The major crops include potatoes, apples, corn, wheat, cherries, soft fruits, wine grapes, concord grapes, and alfalfa.

A major factor contributing to Kennewick's growth was the accessibility of barge, rail, trucking, and air transportation. Following the war and through the next several decades, Kennewick became more diversified with light industry, food processing, and retail. Companies such as Neil F. Lampson Inc., Sandvik Special Metals Corporation, Chevron Chemical Company, Twin City Foods, Cascade Columbia Foods, Union Oil Company, UI Group, Lamb-Weston, Welch Foods Inc., and the *Tri-City Herald* are just

a few of the businesses that have contributed to the growth and development of Kennewick.

More recently, retail trade has had an increasing impact on the Tri-Cities. The downtown Kennewick Parkade features a wide variety of businesses catering to consumers with special needs. The Parkade is known for its high level of personal attention.

In 1969 Columbia Center was constructed in Kennewick. Its central location and easy access by highway soon made the center a popular and profitable business. Columbia Center is the largest covered mall in eastern Washington. Bon Marche, JCPenney, Sears, and Lamonts are the anchor department stores, with another 96 retail outlets within the center. The center recently completed a $15-million expansion project.

Adjacent to Columbia Center are the recently completed Costco and Shopko stores. Also in the immediate vicinity are two smaller malls that provide a wide variety of products and services to Tri-City residents. Cavanaugh's at Columbia Center, a 160-room motor hotel next to Columbia Center, provides overnight accommodations and dining facilities for out-of-town visitors.

Interstate 182, linking Richland with Interstate 82, was completed in February 1986. The new highway improved access among the Tri-Cities and added the Tri-Cities to the

▲ ▲ ▲

Columbia Park in Kennewick is the site of the annual Water Follies Hydroplane Races.

Interstate 82 system, which intersects with Interstate 90 to the north and Interstate 84 to the south.

The most recent addition to Kennewick has been the Tri-Cities Coliseum. Plans for the construction of the 6,000-seat coliseum began in 1987. The facility was completed in April 1989. The Tri-Cities Coliseum was built by Canadian developer Ron Dixon to house a Western Hockey League team. In addition to constructing the facility, Dixon brought his New Westminster Bruins to the Tri-Cities and renamed them the Tri-City Americans. The facility has also been used to host other events such as the Ice Capades, as well as celebrity entertainers.

In 1990 the coliseum hosted the ice hockey preliminaries for the 1990 Goodwill Games. The top eight teams in the world, including the United States and the U.S.S.R. competed for gold, silver, and bronze medals and a chance to compete in the finals held at the Tacoma Dome. The coliseum is just one example of the cooperative public/private enterprise that distinguishes Kennewick and helps to make it a regional leader.

There is more to Kennewick than business. Columbia Park, a 570-acre stretch along the west side of the Columbia River, provides summer recreation for swimmers, boaters, campers, windsurfers, golfers, runners, bikers, and walkers. It is also the location for major group gatherings and the annual Columbia Cup unlimited hydroplane races. In 1990 the races celebrated their 25th year.

The City of Kennewick is committed to developing riverfront areas and has launched a Rivershore Enhancement program to make the Columbia River even more accessible. Plans are under way to lower the dikes, landscape the immediate area, and make more of the river accessible. The project will encourage both public and private development and envisions boardwalks, swimming beaches, boat launch facilities, and expanded park areas south and east of Columbia Park to Clover Island and beyond to Two Rivers Park. Kennewick is working closely with Richland to improve riverfront areas north and west of Columbia Park and within the City of Richland.

▲ ▲ ▲

Pictured here is the public water park in Kennewick.

Rivershore enhancement will not only benefit the Tri-Cities community, but will enhance tourism efforts in the communities that boast 300 days of sunshine.

Growth in Kennewick will also be measured in the development of new residential areas catering to a more sophisticated clientele. Canyon Lakes, Panoramic Heights, and Street of Dreams areas are continuing to grow beyond initial estimates.

The City of Kennewick is committed to growth, while at the same time supporting the existing infrastructure. Continuing to provide excellence in education is a reflection of that commitment. Preparing the community's children to enter the work force or to be successful in higher education is a priority that is supported at all levels in the community.

Kennewick believes that to assure continued growth a commitment must be made to participate in cooperative marketing efforts that are under way in the Tri-Cities. At the same time the City of Kennewick will work to maintain its individual identity within the Tri-Cities. It will focus on supporting businesses already located in Kennewick by helping them grow, by focusing attention on the smaller "boutique" businesses, and by creating an environment that encourages businesses outside the area to consider Kennewick as a good place to relocate. The potential for Kennewick is without limits.

Kadlec Medical Center

▲ ▲ ▲

Kadlec Medical Center is a regional health care provider that offers a broad range of medical services. The medical center is equipped with the latest in sophisticated, state-of-the-art technology and is staffed with highly-trained specialists.

Kadlec Medical Center, located in Richland, is the largest health care facility in the region. Kadlec integrates the latest in medical technology with a highly trained staff and innovative programs that reflect the changing needs of the Tri-Cities and surrounding communities. Kadlec employs more than 600 health care professionals who provide a wide range of medical services. The staff of more than 80 physicians represent 30 specialty areas. Kadlec is dedicated to wellness and improving the availability of health services for southeastern Washington and northeastern Oregon.

One of the most important services Kadlec offers is the Neonatal Intensive Care Unit. Opened in 1982, the unit provides 24-hour nursing care for premature and ill babies. The unit can maintain life support for premature babies until they are able to survive on their own.

Kadlec maintains a specially equipped 12-bed Coronary Care Unit/Intensive Care Unit. It provides close observation and specialized care for the critically ill patient. Computerized cardiac monitors at a centralized nurses' station provide the patient with constant nursing care.

Kadlec's Emergency Department is staffed by emergency-trained nurses and physicians 24 hours per day, seven days per week. Major emergencies are handled through the emergency room with backup support provided by other departments.

The Laboratory Department at Kadlec is also staffed 24 hours per day. This allows for faster diagnosis and treatment.

The Diabetes Learning Center was developed in 1984 to serve the needs of area diabetics and their family members who want to learn

▲ ▲ ▲

LifeLink fitness specialists perform a cardiopulmonary test. LifeLink provides a comprehensive life-style inventory, evaluation, and examination for individuals.

more about managing their illness. The center focuses on teaching clients how to take control of their diabetes and incorporate healthy living habits on a day-to-day basis. Through ongoing education, acceptance of a lifetime of self-management can be achieved. The center also offers a free diabetes screening monthly.

In 1987 Kadlec built the region's first Same-Day Surgery Center for outpatient surgery. The center is easily accessible for patients and their families. Outpatient surgery is the preferred choice for many surgical procedures that previously required an inpatient stay. Roughly 50 percent of all surgeries performed at Kadlec are on an outpatient basis.

LifeLink™ is a personal life-style inventory program created in 1987 to help individuals examine and evaluate their life-styles and educate them about pertinent health-related

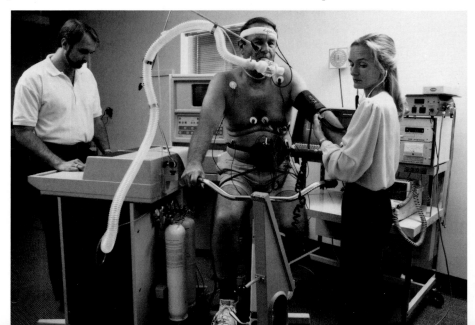

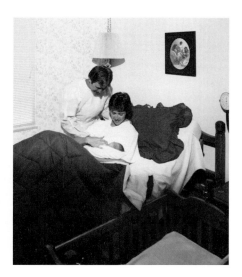

▲ ▲ ▲

Kadlec Birth Center offers a wide range of birthing options for each family's individual needs and preferences.

topics and formulate a personal exercise and nutritional program. LifeLink™ is also available to corporations concerned about their employees' health and provides corporate health screenings, physicals, and mechanisms to change behaviors that reduce performance in the work place.

ElderMED is a free program for senior citizens that began in 1987. The program provides educational programs, insurance counseling, and coordinated access to health care services. ElderMED has more than 7,500 members in Benton/Franklin Counties and outlying areas.

In 1988 Kadlec became the home of the mobile MRI (magnetic resonance imaging) unit, a cooperative venture among the three Tri-City hospitals. Utilizing a super magnet and computer, the MRI creates images without X rays. The MRI provides a clearer view of some internal organs that is superior to other diagnostic methods. Kadlec also has other sophisticated technology such

as nuclear medicine, CAT scanning, ultrasound, and mammography.

Columbia Home Health Services began in 1989 as a joint venture with Our Lady of Lourdes Health Center. The program is designed to provide in-home care for patients.

The Weight Control for Life! program began in 1989 through Kadlec's Outpatient Nutrition Department. The program is designed for people with at least 30 pounds to lose and combines a medically supervised fasting program with an emphasis on life-style modifications, nutrition education, stress management, exercise, and maintenance supervision. Weight Control for Life! helps people lose weight and keep it off.

Lithotripsy, a revolutionary procedure that shatters kidney stones with shock waves, became available at Kadlec in 1990. The recovery from lithotripsy surgery takes only a few days and is one of the major benefits of this new technology. The lithotripsy unit used by Kadlec is shared by several other hospitals in Washington State. It is located in a mobile unit that makes it both accessible and affordable to patients throughout the region.

Kadlec purchased the area's first 55-watt carbon-dioxide laser in 1988. The laser provides an additional tool for physicians, allowing them to perform certain procedures with a precision not possible with traditional surgical practices. The laser is less traumatic for the patient and causes less bleeding, less postoperative pain, and less scarring of the tissue, which leads to a quicker recovery.

The Pastoral Care Department offers emotional and spiritual support to patients and their families. A chaplain is available 24 hours per day.

The Education Department offers a variety of training and self-help classes for patients and the community in general. Kadlec physi-

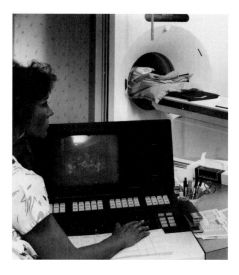

▲ ▲ ▲

Kadlec Medical Center has one of the most advanced CT units produced. The GE 9800 Quick CT Scanner performs studies of head and body tissues with unprecedented detail and accuracy.

cians, nurses, and technicians are constantly updating their skills to provide the best in medical care to their patients.

Kadlec Medical Center had its beginning in 1944 as a government-built facility, providing hospital and industrial medical services to the Hanford Project employees and their families. The hospital, housed then in a sprawling, one-story complex, was named in honor of Lieutenant Colonel Harry R. Kadlec, deputy engineer at Hanford. The present four-story, 144-bed facility was constructed in 1971. The facility has undergone several additions and renovations to better serve the changing needs of the community.

Kadlec Medical Center is continuously planning for the future health care needs of the community and improving the quality of care for the region. Kadlec is a community, nonprofit hospital, governed by a 15-member volunteer board of directors.

Tri-Ports

Tri-Ports

Tri-Ports was originally created by the three ports to work together representing the Tri-Cities in areas where it was most effective to do so. Tri-Ports market the area; jointly attend trade shows; cooperatively advertise in local, regional, national, and international publications; and sponsor an annual local trade show. In addition, Tri-Ports jointly participate in local, state, and regional organizations as a Tri-Cities group, including lobbying efforts. They were also responsible for formally creating Tri-Ports Export Services, more commonly known as Tri-Ex. Tri-Ex is the first export trading company created by ports under Washingtn state law.

"Let us bring the Tri-Cities to you," is the message being sent to international markets by Tri-Ex. Begun in 1988 by the cooperative efforts of the Benton, Kennewick, and Pasco port districts, Tri-Ex helps small- to medium-size businesses in the area explore and develop export opportunities.

Tri-Ex also provides businesses with research and identification of appropriate international markets for local products, assistance in developing those markets, clarification of U.S. and foreign trade regulations, help in making shipping arrangements, assistance in completing export documentation, and acting as the marketing arm for foreign trade through advertising and trade shows. Through Tri-Ex, the Tri-Ports are committed to increasing exports from the region.

Port of Benton

The Port of Benton is committed to industrial development for today and tomorrow. The Port was established in 1958 to promote industrial development and transportation, including general aviation and Columbia River

▲▲▲
The Richland Development Building houses Port offices and eight incubator firms.

marine commerce in Benton County. The Port District encompasses the western three-quarters of Benton County, an area of more than 1,200 square miles.

In the 1960s and 1970s the Port acquired the Richland and Prosser Airports and the Richland and Prosser Industrial Parks. In the early 1980s the Port continued its expansion program by building a second incubator in Prosser and expanding services at its Richland incubator. A third incubator was added in Prosser in 1988.

Richland Industrial Park is a business and industrial campus in a quiet, landscaped setting. Located in the city of Richland, the 290-acre park is easily accessible via city arterials, has a barge dock and slip to handle the heaviest demands of ship-

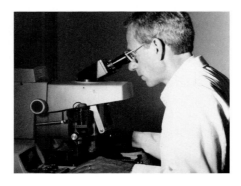

▲▲▲
Matrix Sciences, Inc., a semiconductor research firm, is a Port incubator tenant.

pers, and has more than one mile of Columbia River shoreline available for development.

Richland Development Building, a 38,000-square-foot facility, was the Port's first incubator and provides new or expanding companies short-term leases, competitive rates, and room to grow. It also houses the administrative offices for the Port, as well as Stirling Technology, Medical Billing Systems, Matrix Sciences Inc., and International Technology (IT) Corporation, among others.

Prosser Industrial Park is a 90-acre facility located on the banks of the

▲▲▲
The Hogue Cellars produces award-winning wines at the Port of Benton's Prosser Industrial Park.

Yakima River slightly east of Prosser, with direct interstate access. Another incubator facility is located there, housing The Hogue Cellars Winery.

Prosser Airport, just four miles west of the Industrial Park, in 1988 became the location of the Port's newest incubator, a 3,750-square-foot expandable building that houses

Chukar Cherry Company, Inc. In 1989 the building was expanded to 8,680 square feet.

Richland Skypark provides an airport facility and industrial/commercial space in one convenient location. The 600-acre Skypark in Richland has both existing facilities and land available for warehousing, light manufacturing, and offices. With two 4,000-foot paved and lighted runways, the airport easily accommodates commuter and private planes, and a broad range of general aviation activities. Airborne Express, Schwan's Sales Enterprises, InterroPoint, Baker Aviation, and the U.S. Navy are five of the facility's many tenants.

Port of Kennewick

The Port of Kennewick is a Port of interest for industries looking to relocate or expand. To help sustain and enhance the Tri-Cities, the Port has acquired, zoned, and developed land for industrial use, making it available to local industries and industries from outside the area. The Port has industrial properties in seven locations within the district. An industrial port, the Port of Kennewick encompasses 49 shoreline miles of the Columbia River. It also has access to two transcontinental railroads, a full-service regional airport, and major interstate freeways.

The Port of Kennewick was established in 1915 and began an era of economic development that continues today. By the mid-1940s the Port had acquired Clover Island, a large natural island. Over the years the Port expanded its boundaries to encompass about one-third of Benton County. The late 1950s and the 1960s brought an era of significant growth. Five major chemical plants, several large food-processing plants, a major metallurgical plant, cold-storage facilities, and boating facilities were all

built and became operational during this period. The 1970s and 1980s have focused attention on targeting new businesses to the Tri-Cities and assisting local businesses in getting off to a good start.

One of the methods used for encouraging industrial growth is the Port's development program involving incubator facilities. Incubators provide space and services at a low

▲ ▲ ▲
A worker at the Chevron Chemical plant, located in the Port of Kennewick.

cost to encourage company growth, development, and expansion. Three such facilities are located at the Port's Oak Street Industrial Site, which contains more than 100 acres with 1,800

▲▲▲
The Port of Kennewick, at the Oak Street site, is the location for Sandvik Special Metals-Titanium Sports Division.

feet of waterfront. The incubators house Perseus Gourmet Products, Amera Cosmetics, Sandvik Titanium Sports Division, Innovative Technology Laboratories, and Ag Engineering & Development Company. A fourth incubator is located at Vista Field for utilization by high-technology industries and electronics manufacturers, including the rapidly expanding Staveley Instruments.

Hedges Industrial Site contains more than 80 available acres in two parcels, all zoned for industrial use. This site has 4,800 feet of waterfront. Much of this area has been developed. Finley Industrial Site contains more than 165 available acres in three parcels all zoned for industrial use. This site has 1,400 feet of waterfront. Hover Industrial Site contains 197

acres and is exceptionally suited for heavy industrial use. The site has 4,069 feet of waterfront. Plymouth Industrial Site contains 265 acres and is zoned for industrial use. The site has approximately 9,000 feet of waterfront.

Clover Island, which serves as the port's headquarters, is commercial in nature, rather than industrial. Most of the island is developed with the exception of three acres with 800 feet of waterfront. Clover Island also houses Cedars Pier 1 Restaurant, Clover Island Inn, Metz Marina, the Clover Island Yacht Club, a U.S. Coast Guard station, and a public boat-launching ramp.

Port of Pasco

The Port of Pasco is a municipal corporation that was organized in 1940 to utilize barge transportation on the Columbia River as a means of transporting grain to markets at seacoast terminals and beyond. Services at the original marine terminal were expanded over the years to include facilities for petroleum handling and storage. In 1959 the Port purchased a World War II U.S. Army depot, now known as Big Pasco Industrial Center. In 1963 the Port took over the former World War II U.S. Naval Air Station in Pasco and renamed it the Tri-Cities Airport. In 1976 the

▲▲▲
Big Pasco Industrial Center on the banks of the majestic Columbia River.

container terminal center was established to handle the steadily increasing volume of import and export cargo.

The completion by the Port of Pasco in 1986 of the expansion and modernization program at the Tri-Cities Airport marked a new chapter in air travel for the entire Columbia Basin region. The greatly expanded airline terminal area and new airfield improvements were well timed to serve a large growth in airline passengers. The third-busiest commercial airport in Washington is also designed to more easily take advantage of anticipated future growth. Second-level, all-weather passenger loading facilities will very likely be the next development to meet travelers' needs. As traffic grows, the terminal can easily be expanded without serious disruption.

The Tri-Cities Airport has thrived in the era of airline deregulation, a result of congressional action in 1978 that allows airlines to enter or exit communities at will. A major development in 1987 was the decision by a new regional airline to establish its corporate headquarters and maintenance and training base at the Tri-Cities Airport. NPA, Inc., flying as United Express, began operations in Pasco and now has more than 500

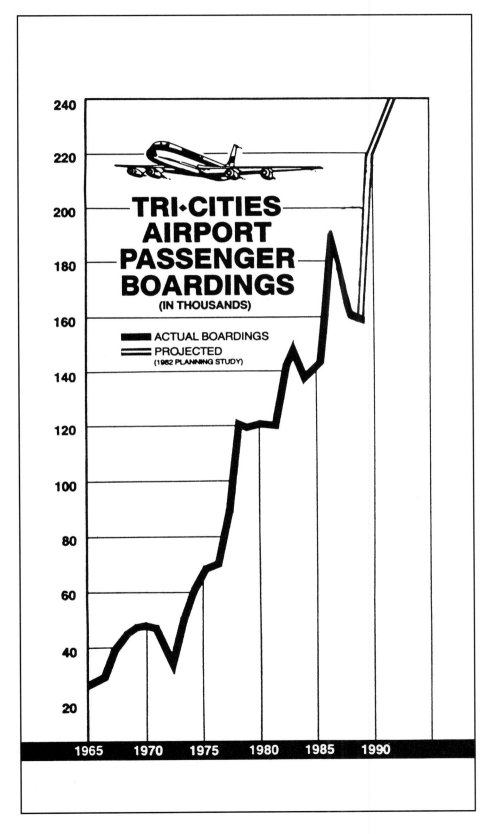

TRI·CITIES AIRPORT PASSENGER BOARDINGS
(IN THOUSANDS)

■ ACTUAL BOARDINGS
≡ PROJECTED
(1982 PLANNING STUDY)

▲ ▲ ▲
Passenger traffic at the Tri-Cities Airport has tripled since 1975.

employees with more than half based in the Tri-Cities.

The air-freight industry is another target for growth. The 1980s have seen the birth of many overnight mail and package express carriers. The Port built a specially designed air-freight facility located southeast of the passenger terminal.

In addition to aviation-related facilities, the Tri-Cities Airport features a 90-acre tract west of the terminal that has been planned for commercial and light-industrial development and a hotel site, a 200-acre industrial site northeast of the airfield, and a diversified industrial park east of the airport.

The marine terminal provides year-round barge service to and from Pacific Coast ports. The 28-acre facility handles the largest bulk cargo tonnage of any area on the Columbia River above the Portland/Vancouver districts. The facility houses a 20-million-gallon petroleum tank farm, a 500,000-bushel grain elevator, and a bulk cement plant.

Big Pasco Industrial Center has 600 acres of land with several miles of railroad tracks and streets and 1.7 million square feet of buildings. The eight buildings that make up the major industrial space are designed to work equally well for both truck and rail shipments. They are built with a heavy frame construction over solid concrete floors and are divided into four bays with covered docks.

The container terminal center dock facilities include a certified 36-ton whirley crane and a substantial pool of for-lease containers. Specially designed barges have been placed in service on the Columbia River to handle the Port of Pasco's container shipments.

▲ ▲ ▲

The Ice Harbor Dam dedication on May 9, 1962, included this special flotilla of boats through the navigation lock. The lock is 675 feet long, 86 feet wide, and has a maximum lift of 103 feet. The lock's chamber holds about 43 million gallons of water—enough to fill a line of bathtubs stretched end to end from Ice Harbor Dam to San Francisco. Courtesy, U.S. Army Corps of Engineers, Walla Walla District

Patrons

The following individuals, companies, and organizations have made a valuable commitment to the quality of this publication. Windsor Publications and the Tri-City Industrial Development Council gratefully acknowledge their participation in *Tri-Cities: The Mid-Columbia Hub.*

American National Bank*
Battelle Northwest Laboratories*
BCS Richland, Inc. (BCSR)*
Benton County Public Utility District (PUD)*
Chevron Chemical Company*
City of Kennewick*
City of Richland*
George A. Grant, Inc.*
Kadlec Medical Center*
Kaiser Engineers Hanford*
Kennewick General Hospital*
KONA AM/FM Tri-Cities Communications*
Neil F. Lampson Inc.*
Our Lady of Lourdes Health Center*
Perseus Gourmet Products*
Sandvik Special Metals Corporation*
Tri-City Herald*
Tri-City Industrial Development Council*
Tri-Ports*
United Express/NPA, Inc.*
Washington Public Power Supply System*
Washington State University at Tri-Cities*
Westinghouse Electric Corporation*

*Partners in Progress of *Tri-Cities: The Mid-Columbia Hub.* The histories of these companies and organizations appear in Chapter 7, beginning on page 106.

Bibliography

Anderson, D. Victor. *Illusions of Power, A History of the Washington Public Power Supply System.* New York: Praeger Publishers, 1985.

Beardsley, Paul. *The Long Road to Self-Government, The History of Richland, Washington, 1943-1968.* Kennewick, WA: Tri-City Herald 1968.

Benton County, Washington—A Glimpse of the Past. Kennewick, WA: Benton County Historical and Pioneer Association, 1967.

Christodoulou, A.P. *Conversion of Nuclear Facilities from Military to Civilian Uses, A Case Study in Hanford, Washington.* New York: Praeger Publishers, 1970.

Cummings, Bernice. *History of the Three Wallulas and Area, 1811-1988.* College Place, WA: Color Press, 1988.

Davis, Jean Carol. *See South-Central Washington, A Sunday Drive Guide.* Kennewick, WA: Lea Jarvis and Co., 1982.

Edinger, Vera. *The Hanford Story—A Success Story Against Tremendous Odds.* Seattle, WA: Washington PUD Association, 1964.

Groves, Leslie R. *Now It Can Be Told, The Story of the Manhattan Project.* New York: Harper & Row, 1962.

Hanford, Yesterday, Today and Tomorrow. Richland, WA: third edition, 1977.

Harris, Mary Powell. *Goodbye White Bluffs.* Yakima, WA: Franklin Press, 1972.

Hartman, Maude, ed. *History of Benton City, Washington, 1853-1959.* Benton City, WA: 1959.

Holsted, P.G., and F.W. Albaugh. *Hanford Capabilities.* Richland, WA: U.S. Atomic Energy Commission, 1964.

Hope, Nelson W. *Atomic Town.* New York: Comet Press Books, 1954.

Jensen, Ernest Z., with Richard W. Swanson. *Bomber Mania, The History of Richland High School Basketball 1953-1980.* Everett, WA: Patrick's Printing, 1980.

Klindworth, Edward C. *The Beginnings of Connell.* Portland, OR: 1966.

Lewty, Peter J. *To the Columbia Gateway, The Oregon Railway and the Northern Pacific, 1879-1884.* Pullman, WA: Washington State University Press, 1987.

Loeb, Paul. *Nuclear Culture, Living and Working in the World's Largest Atomic Complex.* New York: Coward, McCann & Geoghegan, Inc., 1982.

Mahoney, Pearl M. *Prosser the Home Town.* Prosser, WA: Prosser Printing Co., 1950.

Meyer, Bette E., with Barbara Kubik. *Ainsworth, a Railroad Town.* Fairfield, WA: Ye Galleon Press, 1983.

Oberst, Walter A. *Railroads, Reclamation and the River, A History of Pasco.* Pasco, WA: Franklin County Historical Society, 1978.

———, and Ralph Smith. *Pasco, 100 Years in Pictures.* Kennewick, WA: Tri-Ad Printing, 1983.

Parker, Martha Berry. *Kin-i-wak, Kenewick, Tehe, Kennewick.* Fairfield, WA: Ye Galleon Press, 1986.

———. *Tales of Richland, White Bluffs and Hanford 1805-1943.* Fairfield, WA: Ye Galleon Press, 1979.

Pendergrass, Bonnie Baack. *Public Power, Politics and Technology in the Eisenhower and Kennewick Years, The Hanford Dual-Purpose Reactor Controversy, 1956-1962.* New York: Arno Press, 1979.

Pugnetti, Frances Taylor. *Tiger by the Tail, 25 Years with the Stormy Tri-City Herald.* Tacoma, WA: Mercury Press, 1975.

Relander, Click. *Drummers and Dreamers.* Caldwell, ID: The Caxton Printers, 1956.

Rice, David G. *Cultural Resources at Hanford.* Richland, WA: Washington Public Power Supply System.

Richland, Washington, A Study of Economic Impact. Walla Walla, WA: Whitman College Economics and Business Administration Department, May 1955.

Sanger, S.L. *Hanford and the Bomb: an Oral History of World War II.* Seattle, WA: Living History Press, 1989.

Silver Anniversary Steering Committee. *Alive: Richland and the Hanford Project.* Kennewick, WA: Advance Advertising, Inc., 1983.

Smyth, H.D. *A General Account of the Development of Methods of Using Atomic Energy for Military Purposes Under Auspices of the United States Government 1940-1945.* Washington, D.C.: Government Printing Office, August 1945.

Thompson, Margaret. *Benton County, Washington.* Prosser, WA: 1954.

U.S. Department of the Interior. *Final Environmental Statement, Proposed Columbia Basin Project, Washington.* Bureau of Reclamation, Pacific Northwest Region, 1976.

Van Arsdol, Ted. *Desert Boom and Bust.* Vancouver, WA: 1970.

———. *Hanford, the Big Secret.* Pasco, WA: The *Columbia Basin News,* 1958.

Vogel, Leo F. *Years Plowed Under.* Spokane, WA: University Press, 1977.

MANUSCRIPTS AND THESES

Deutschmann, Paul John. *Federal City, A Study of the Administration of Richland, Washington, Atomic Energy Commission Community.* Eugene, OR: thesis presented to University of Oregon Department of Political Science.

Fleischer, Christian Calmeyer. *The Tri-City Nuclear Industrial Council and the Economic Diversification of the Tri-Cities, Washington, 1963-1974.* Pullman, WA: M.A. Thesis, Washington State University Department of History.

Hales, Marjorie. *The History of Pasco, Washington, to 1915.* Pullman, WA: M.A., Washington State University, 1964.

Meyer, Delbert. *A Study of the Development of the Tri-Cities.* Kennewick, WA: thesis, 1959 (unpublished).

Van Arsdol, Ted. *The Birth of Hanford.* World War II era (unpublished).

Index